TRUST
360

How Authentic
Leaders Build Trust,
Inspire Teams, and Drive
Success in an Ever-Changing World

By Ivan Radovic

Table of Contents

Acknowledgments

This book would not have been possible without the people who challenged me, inspired me, and walked with me, both in life and leadership.

To my children, Marko and Ivanna, you are my greatest teachers. Watching you grow, question, and pursue your own paths has reminded me again and again what trust, resilience, and purpose really mean. You are the reason I strive to lead with integrity and heart.

To my parents, thank you for the values you passed down and the sacrifices you made so I could chase my dreams far from home. Your strength and example continue to guide me.

To someone who profoundly reminded me that some doors never fully close, and that trust, when rekindled, can bring light to places we thought were long behind us. Thank you for helping me rediscover a piece of myself I thought was lost.

To my longtime business partner, Brian MacClaren, thank you for 21 years of collaboration, trust, and shared vision. Your steadfast support, especially during the writing of this book, has been invaluable.

To my NOVACES team—you are the embodiment of what this book stands for. Thank you for your courage to embrace new ideas, for bringing these concepts to life in the field, and for holding me accountable to lead the way I write about here. Your dedication inspires me daily.

To the editors and creative partners who helped bring this manuscript to life, thank you for your thoughtful questions, sharp eyes, and honest feedback. You didn't just improve the words; you helped shape the message.

To the Entrepreneurs' Organization (EO) community, thank you for providing a space to reflect, grow, and explore the deeper questions of leadership and life. The wisdom, friendship, and authenticity I've experienced through countless conversations, forums, and learning events have profoundly shaped the path that led to this book. I am deeply grateful to everyone who has shared their insights and journeys along the way.

To the mentors, clients, and partners along the way, thank you for showing me what works, what doesn't, and what's possible when trust becomes the foundation.

And finally, to you—the reader. Whether you're leading a team, building a company, or searching for your own voice in a noisy world, I hope these pages offer you something real. The journey continues. And I'm honored to have walked part of it with you.

Trust as the Compass

I didn't set out to write a leadership book. I set out to tell the truth.

For over two decades, I have worked alongside executives, government leaders, nonprofit founders, and startup visionaries, helping them navigate the complexities of leadership in environments that often feel anything but predictable. What I have seen, repeatedly, is that the best strategy, the smartest plan, or the most advanced technology means little if trust is missing. Without it, teams fracture. Culture stagnates. Innovation stalls. But with trust? Even the most daunting challenges become stepping stones.

My own journey has taken me across continents and industries. I come from a multicultural background shaped by resilience, wartime survival stories, and a belief in the power of education and service. I have built companies, advised federal agencies, helped lead disaster recovery efforts, and facilitated culture change in institutions with lifespans longer than most countries. Through it all, one principle remained constant: *people follow trust, not titles.*

One of my business acquaintances, a sharp and accomplished woman, once asked me, somewhat skeptically, "How can someone coming from Eastern Europe write a book about trust?" I smiled and told her, "That's exactly why I need to write it." I arrived in the United States in 1991 from the former Yugoslavia, just as the region was descending into a brutal war. What little trust had remained in society was shattered, replaced by betrayal, fear, and atrocity. I came here to start over. Although I had studied English before arriving, it was far from perfect. I worked multiple jobs while putting myself through college, learning not just how to survive, but how to grow and lead in a country that became my new home. That experience didn't just give me a fresh start; it gave me a deep understanding of what broken trust looks like and how vital it is to restore and protect it. The truth is, many organizations today still carry that same kind of hidden fracture, one that can only be healed through trust-centered leadership.

This book, *Trust 360: How Authentic Leaders Build Trust, Inspire Teams and Drive Success in an Ever-Changing World*, is not a theoretical exercise. It is a field guide drawn from lived experience, for leaders navigating a world where change is relentless, technology impacts every interaction, and people yearn for authenticity. It is for those who want to lead not through control, but through character.

In these pages, I share lessons learned the hard way and the hopeful way. Stories from inside boardrooms and field operations. Missteps I made. Breakthroughs I witnessed. You will see how servant leadership, when anchored in trust and guided by clarity, can become not just a philosophy but a strategy, one that drives measurable results and enduring loyalty.

My hope is that this book helps leaders at all stages, especially those with formal education and experience behind them, but with a hunger to grow, to reimagine what effective leadership looks like. It is my belief that leadership is no longer about having all the answers. It is about asking the right questions, showing up with integrity, and creating an environment where others can rise.

As you read, you will find practical tools, case studies, and frameworks, such as Trust 360, the 80/20 lens on leadership, RCC (Relationship, Capability, and Credibility) for business development, and Artificial Intelligence (AI), to help you cultivate a future-forward mindset rooted in service. But more than that, I hope you find encouragement. Because leading with trust is not always the easiest path, but it is the one that lasts.

Welcome to the journey.

PART I Past:

The Journey to Trust-Based Leadership

CHAPTER 1

Embracing Trust-Based Leadership for Current and Future Leaders

Like all journeys, mine began with turbulence.
The year was 2004, when my leadership journey began.

In 2004, I embarked on a journey to start a consulting business with four other partners. Some of them were long-time acquaintances, while others were relatively new to me. From the outset, there were clear signs that we weren't fully aligned. Days, then months, were consumed in deliberations over how to structure the ownership. Disagreements over how to run the business and which services to offer to various industries pulled us in different directions. It felt disorganized, a common occurrence in startups, but still a challenge. We were all based in New Orleans, and as many of you know, August 2005 brought Hurricane Katrina, which devastated the city. Our fledgling client base was disrupted. Businesses either stopped operating or were in the throes of rebuilding. It seemed we were doomed to fail. To compound the adversity, trust issues among the partners began to surface. The disaster scattered us across the country, and the physical distance only magnified our difficulties.

Fortuitously, we secured a large contract that jump-started our business. Growth followed, but it necessitated reducing our partnership to two. The process of buying out partners coincided with a realization of high staff turnover. Despite our belief that we were transparent and communicative, it became evident that our team didn't trust us, leading them to seek opportunities elsewhere. This was our wake-up call: we were not effectively serving our people, and as a result, they struggled to serve our clients. We also faced challenges with our partner companies on various projects. What were we doing wrong? We weren't serving our people effectively and were failing as leaders to the highly educated professionals who composed our workforce. Our employees were not inspired to stay with our company.

This realization spurred a change. We committed to becoming servant leaders. The transition was not without its learning curve, but it became clear that trust between us and our team was paramount. One of the first steps we took was deceptively simple: we began referring to our employees as team members. At first glance, it might seem like a minor linguistic adjustment. But in practice, it represented a foundational shift from managing employees to empowering people. The word "employee" carries a transactional connotation, whereas "team member" speaks to shared purpose, mutual accountability, and respect. It helped create an experience where people felt they belonged and were part of something bigger than themselves.

This subtle change in language catalyzed a much deeper transformation in how we led, supported, and communicated throughout the organization. It reinforced the idea that every person mattered and that their voices, contributions, and well-being were integral to our success. The ethos of trust and inclusion began at hiring and extended to every department, from human resources to operations to administrative support. Our internal staff reframed their roles as enablers of team success, and we, as partners, embraced the responsibility of servant leadership.

The impact was measurable. Before this shift, our annual retention rate hovered around 60%. Many team members viewed the company as a stepping stone rather than a place to grow. But as trust deepened and the sense of belonging took root, something remarkable happened: people stayed. Just a few years into this cultural shift, our retention rate climbed to 94%. We did not need gimmicks or grand gestures, just a real commitment to putting people first.

Today, as we celebrate the 21-year mark as a company, we are proud to have numerous team members with over 10 years of tenure, and several with over 15 years. This kind of long-term commitment is rare in our industry and is a direct reflection of the trust, purpose, and community we have built together. In fact, some of our most talented hires have come not from job postings, but from conversations, team members referring close friends, former colleagues, and even family, because they believe in what we are building. That kind of endorsement cannot be bought; it is earned through years of authentic leadership and meaningful relationships. This was the beginning of our ongoing journey to elevate servant leadership, one that we recommit to every single day.

Our commitment to a culture of trust-based leadership transcends the boundaries of our organization, influencing not only our internal team dynamics but also shaping our interactions with clients, prospective clients, companies we partner with on projects, and all business discussions. This outward extension of trust-based principles is a testament to our belief that the essence of leadership is not confined to the corridors of our offices but is evident in every engagement and relationship we nurture.

We approach each client and prospective client with the same ethos of transparency, integrity, and support that we champion internally. This means actively listening to their needs, understanding their challenges, and consistently delivering on our promises. By doing so, we not only build strong, trustworthy relationships but also set a standard for reliability and excellence that distinguishes us in the competitive landscape.

Our partnerships on projects are equally infused with this trust-centric philosophy. We believe that collaboration, underpinned by mutual respect and honesty, is the key to achieving shared success. This approach extends to all our business discussions, where we strive to be as open and forthright as possible, fostering an atmosphere of mutual trust and understanding that facilitates smoother negotiations and more fruitful outcomes.

It is important to clarify that when we refer to Trust 360 in this context, we are not alluding to any concept used by IT security companies or in other industries. Instead, Trust 360, as presented in this book, signifies a holistic approach to fostering trust in all organizational relationships—between leaders and team members, with clients, suppliers, and strategic partners. It represents an all-directional commitment to transparency, empathy, and accountability. This distinction underscores the leadership-centric nature of Trust 360, positioning trust as the bedrock of organizational culture and success, far removed from any technical or compliance-driven definition of the term.

As our commitment to trust deepened, we also began integrating frameworks that could reinforce it in day-to-day practice. One such framework is the 80/20 rule, also known as the Pareto Principle. Traditionally, this principle suggests that 80% of outcomes come from 20% of inputs, but we interpreted it through a human lens. Drawing from the work of Dan Sullivan and Dr. Benjamin Hardy in *10x Is Easier Than 2x*, we observed that most people typically spend only 20% of their time on tasks they enjoy, excel at, and believe truly matter. The rest is consumed by routine work that may be necessary but doesn't energize them or fully utilize their talents.

We saw an opportunity, and a responsibility, as leaders to flip that equation. By identifying the 20% of activities where each team member shines, and empowering them to spend more time there, we created a workplace where trust was not just a value, it was a structure. People felt seen, supported, and purposeful. Productivity improved, but more importantly, so did morale and innovation.

This concept will be explored more fully in a later chapter, but it is important to recognize here that Trust 360 and the 80/20 principle are deeply interconnected. Trust allows leaders to give people the freedom to focus on what they do best. The 80/20 principle helps us identify what that "best" looks like and how to design roles and responsibilities around it.

This comprehensive chapter forms a foundational guide for current and future leaders. It illustrates how embracing trust-based leadership principles can overcome challenges, align a team towards a common goal, and drive sustainable growth. Through these teachings, leaders are equipped to foster a culture of trust, integrity, and mutual support, ensuring their organizations thrive in today's dynamic business landscape.

We have embraced the philosophy of inspiring our team to engage in work that aligns with their strengths and interests. This alignment not only boosts performance and job satisfaction but also fosters innovation and a deep sense of belonging. However, we also recognize that growth often happens just outside the comfort zone. That is why we encourage our team members to stretch their capabilities by taking on new challenges that expand their skill sets, supported by a foundation of trust. By balancing alignment with opportunities for development, we have created an environment where motivation, productivity, and personal growth flourish, ultimately driving meaningful impact across the organization.

In the realm of leadership, trust is not merely a soft skill; it's a fundamental element that shapes the culture, performance, and success of an organization. This chapter delves into the principles of trust-based leadership, drawing on insights from a leadership workshop that highlighted the critical role trust plays in fostering a thriving workplace.

At the heart of trust-based leadership lies the understanding that leadership is not about wielding power or enforcing control. Instead, it's about building relationships, understanding, and mutual respect among all members of the organization. This approach contrasts sharply with traditional leadership models, which often focus on hierarchy, command, and control.

A practical expression of trust-based leadership is the thoughtful use of focus and delegation. Rather than trying to do everything themselves, effective leaders concentrate their energy on the few actions that create the greatest impact and entrust others with responsibilities that allow them to grow. This approach not only amplifies results but also signals confidence in the team's capabilities, strengthening trust through shared ownership and accountability.

Another critical component is aligning personal and organizational goals. When leaders and their teams work towards shared objectives, they create a sense of unity and purpose. This alignment not only enhances performance but also builds a strong foundation of trust, as team members feel their contributions are valued and aligned with their personal aspirations.

Trust-based leadership emphasizes the importance of servant leadership. Unlike traditional leadership, which often prioritizes the leader's success and authority, servant leadership focuses on the growth and well-being of team members. By putting the needs of their teams first, leaders can create a supportive environment that encourages innovation, collaboration, and trust.

One of the most helpful frameworks for understanding servant leadership was first articulated by Robert Greenleaf and later refined by many others. These principles provide a practical way to evaluate how we show up as leaders—not as abstract ideals, but as daily practices that shape our teams and organizations.

Core Principles of Servant Leadership:

- **Active listening**: Giving full attention to others, seeking to understand before being understood
- **Empathy**: Placing yourself in another's perspective and experience
- **Healing**: Recognizing and addressing emotional wounds within yourself and others
- **Self-awareness**: Understanding your strengths, limitations, and how you affect those around you
- **Persuasion**: Leading through influence and consensus, rather than positional authority
- **Conceptualization**: Seeing the bigger picture and helping others connect their work to the long-term vision
- **Foresight**: Anticipating consequences and learning from past experiences to guide present decisions
- **Stewardship**: Acting as a responsible caretaker of the resources and trust placed in your hands.
- **Commitment to the growth of people**: Investing in the personal and professional development of team members.

- **Building community**: Creating an environment of belonging, collaboration, and shared purpose.

You don't have to master all of these at once. In fact, many leaders discover that they naturally lean into some more than others. What matters is the willingness to reflect, adapt, and grow. Throughout this book, we will return to these principles again and again, not as theory, but as guideposts you can apply in real situations.

Finally, trust-based leadership requires leaders to be vulnerable, open, and authentic. By sharing their own challenges and learning from failures, leaders can create a culture of openness and mutual support. This vulnerability fosters trust and strengthens relationships within the team, leading to increased engagement, loyalty, and performance.

Trust-based leadership is not a quick fix or a one-size-fits-all solution. It requires a commitment to personal growth, empathy, and a genuine desire to serve others. By embracing these principles, leaders can transform their organizations, creating a culture of trust, collaboration, and excellence that drives long-term success.

CHAPTER 2

The Transformation to Servant Leadership

I n the next stage of our story, we discovered what it truly means to lead by serving, and why not every leader is ready for that shift. This chapter delves into the transformative process of shifting from traditional leadership paradigms to a servant leadership model, highlighting the challenges, strategies, and outcomes of this transition.

Once we had steadied the company after those early storms and laid the foundation of trust, it felt like the right moment to build a more formal leadership layer. We believed that trust was now strong enough to support structure, and that structure would help us scale. Our guiding assumption was simple: those who had been in the industry longest had earned the right to lead. Experience, we thought, equaled leadership.

At first, this seemed natural. Some of these leaders embraced their roles wholeheartedly, modeling humility, lifting up their teams, and weaving servant leadership into the fabric of the company. But others revealed a different pattern. They wore the title but not the responsibility. Rather than serving, they protected their turf. Rather than empowering, they controlled. Their focus was not on building trust or enabling growth, but on securing their own position.

The results showed quickly. Junior team members began to express frustrations. Some peers on the management team quietly admitted they were losing confidence in certain colleagues. Instead of reinforcing the culture of trust we had worked so hard to establish, we were creating fractures. The truth became clear: experience alone is not the same as servant leadership. Trust cannot thrive when leaders are chosen for tenure rather than temperament.

The solution required courage. We made the difficult choice to restructure. First, we completely flattened the organization. For a few years, we removed the middle layer of management, making it clear that every team member could speak directly with anyone, including us as partners. Communication became quicker, accountability sharper, and trust began to regrow.

Later, when we reintroduced a leadership layer, it was with new clarity. This time, titles would go only to those who *breathed* servant leadership—leaders who listened first, served first, and saw their role as enabling others. The difference was striking. Trust deepened, alignment strengthened, and the organization became far more resilient.

That restructuring marked a turning point. It was the first time we realized that servant leadership cannot be assumed; it must be intentional. It also taught us that building trust is not enough—leaders must sustain it through service. This was the true beginning of our path to servant leadership.

Recognizing the Need for Change

The path to recognizing the need for change in leadership style is often fraught with discomfort and denial. For many leaders, including myself, the hardest pill to swallow is realizing that our leadership approach, which we've meticulously crafted and taken pride in, might be the very source of our team's and organization's struggles. The road towards this recognition is not just about identifying shortcomings in our methods; it's deeply personal, challenging our self-perception and the identity we've built as leaders.

Acknowledging failures is particularly challenging for leaders because it confronts our deeply held beliefs about our competencies and leadership styles. For years, I took pride in being hands-on, making my presence felt in every decision and every room. My intention was to steer my team towards excellence, believing that my direct involvement was crucial for success. This approach, however, had its pitfalls. I wanted my word to be the most important, thinking this would ensure alignment and efficiency.

One example that stands out was during a major client project where we were developing a new performance management framework. Several team members had proposed innovative approaches that could have improved efficiency, but instead of letting them lead, I overruled their ideas and directed the solution myself. We delivered on time, but the outcome was uninspired. Worse, the team felt their contributions didn't matter. The result was compliance, not commitment.

Unbeknownst to me, moments like these were leading us toward stagnation. By trying to control the process and ensure my voice was always central, I unintentionally stifled creativity and discouraged autonomy.

Like many leaders, I was trapped in the illusion of control. The belief that being deeply involved in every aspect of the operation and making the final decisions was a hallmark of strong leadership. This mindset is not uncommon; many leaders equate leadership with control, oversight, and having the final say. The reality, however, is that this approach can lead to micromanagement, eroding trust and stifling the growth and development of the team. It also sends an unintended message: that those working with you are not capable of handling responsibility on their own. Over time, this makes talented people feel inept, disempowered, and less willing to contribute their best ideas.

My Journey to Self-Realization

My journey towards recognizing the need for change was gradual and, at times, painful. Feedback from my team, which initially felt like personal attacks, began to paint a picture I could no longer ignore. They would say things like, *"You don't need to be in every meeting. We can handle it,"* or *"Sometimes it feels like you've already decided before we start talking."* Others admitted, *"I don't always feel trusted to run with my ideas,"* or *"It's hard to grow when every decision comes back to you."* At first, I dismissed these comments as misunderstandings or oversensitivity, but as the themes repeated, I realized the issue was not their perception; it was my behavior. I came to see that my need to be involved in everything and have the final word was not a sign of effective leadership; it was a barrier to our success.

The transition from denial to acceptance is a crucial step in a leader's evolution. It requires humility, introspection, and the willingness to change. For me, it involved letting go of the ego and the deeply ingrained belief that my leadership style was beyond reproach. It was a process of unlearning and relearning, of opening myself up to feedback and viewing it not as criticism but as the key to unlocking a more effective and inclusive leadership approach.

My experience is far from unique. Like many leaders, I operated for years under the misconception that I was steering my ship adeptly, unaware that my leadership style might be the very storm causing the turbulence. The realization that my leadership approach was failing was a pivotal moment for me; it was humbling and deeply personal. It is a crossroads where every leader, myself included, must choose between continuing down a path of self-deception and stagnation or embracing the discomfort of change for the growth and betterment of their team and organization.

The path to recognizing the need for change is complex and multifaceted. It's about confronting uncomfortable truths, challenging our perceptions of leadership, and embracing vulnerability. This process is not just about improving as a leader; it's about changing our approach to leadership in a way that serves the greater good of our teams and our organizations. It marks the beginning of a shift towards a more servant-oriented leadership style, where the focus transitions from commanding to serving, from speaking to listening, and from leading to empowering.

The Essence of Servant Leadership: Embracing Autonomy and Learning from Failure

In my journey towards servant leadership, I encountered pivotal moments that reshaped my understanding of what it truly means to serve and lead. One such moment came when I stopped answering every question in team meetings and instead asked, "What do you think is the best path forward?"

The shift was small, but it revealed how much my team wanted to be heard and how quickly they rose to the occasion when given space. Rooted in the intention to prioritize the needs of others, servant leadership diverges significantly from traditional leadership models that place the leader at the apex of the organizational hierarchy. This approach is characterized by a deep commitment to the growth, well-being, and satisfaction of team members, with the belief that success naturally follows when the team's needs are met. Key attributes of servant leadership include empathy, active listening, stewardship, and a dedication to the personal development of team members.

One of my earliest lessons in this came when I hired the company's first administrative assistant. I was eager to delegate, but when her work didn't look exactly like how I would have done it, I grew frustrated. Instead of coaching her through it, I quietly took back many of the tasks and started doing them myself. At the time, I told myself I was saving time and protecting quality. In reality, I was undermining her confidence and robbing her of the chance to learn and grow. That moment revealed how easily "helping" can slide into controlling.

At first, I didn't see it. I thought my intervention was harmless—maybe even helpful. But slowly, I began to notice subtle shifts in her behavior. She stopped offering suggestions. She began checking in with me constantly before moving forward. When decisions needed to be made, her first instinct was to ask, "What do you want me to do?" I had created a dependency without realizing it. What I thought was protecting the company's standards was, in fact, sending the message that her contributions were not good enough unless they matched mine.

The realization came to me in stages. I remember one particular day when she hesitated over a routine task, waiting for me to give instructions. The frustration I felt in that moment bounced back on me like a mirror: I was the reason she lacked confidence. My attempts to "help" had taken away her chance to develop her own judgment and grow into the role. It dawned on me that I was not only hindering her growth but also setting limits on the future of the team. If I remained the bottleneck, nothing would scale beyond my own capacity.

Eventually, the truth became impossible to ignore. Through her quiet disengagement and later through candid feedback from other team members, I came to see that I was undervaluing the very people I had hired for their talents and perspectives. That was a humbling moment, one that forced me to reexamine what it really meant to lead. Servant leadership, I realized, is not about swooping in to fix every problem. It is about creating the conditions where others can step into their full potential, even if that means things get messy, imperfect, or done differently than I would have done them.

So I made a shift. I began to explain the "why" behind tasks instead of dictating the "how." I encouraged her to take risks, even small ones, and I resisted the urge to jump in when she struggled. I provided feedback with patience, not frustration, and celebrated progress rather than perfection. Over time, the team grew more confident and capable, making decisions without my prompting, solving problems in their own way, and even suggesting improvements I had never considered. Watching team members step into their strengths was a turning point for me.

That experience reshaped my understanding of leadership. It taught me that trust is not built by holding on tightly but by letting go with intention. Empowering others means resisting the impulse to control and instead offering guidance, encouragement, and space to grow. It is not about proving that I can do the work better; it is about proving that I believe others can.

Shifting my leadership style involved embracing the true essence of servant leadership, where leaders act more as coaches and mentors. Instead of assuming I knew what motivated my team, I began asking intentional questions: What part of your work excites you most? Which tasks feel draining? Where do you want to grow next?

I also paid attention to patterns; who naturally took the lead in problem-solving, who thrived under pressure, and who showed creativity in areas outside their formal role. By combining what they told me with what I observed, I gained a clearer picture of each person's strengths and interests. From there, I looked for ways to align their roles with those qualities. For example, assigning the detail-oriented analyst the responsibility of refining our reporting systems, or asking the team member who loves client interaction to take on onboarding. The focus turned toward creating opportunities that matched people's natural talents with real organizational needs, thereby increasing motivation and satisfaction. This approach required a careful balance between offering support and allowing room for autonomy, encouraging team members to explore their potential and contribute uniquely to the organization's success.

To deepen this understanding, we later turned to Patrick Lencioni's framework of the *Six Types of Working Genius*. We had our entire company take the survey, and the results were eye-opening. Suddenly, we could see not just individual strengths, but how the mix of talents shaped team dynamics. Some excelled in Wonder and Invention, sparking ideas and possibilities. Others thrived in Discernment and Galvanizing, bringing intuition and momentum to move things forward. Still others shone in Enablement and Tenacity, ensuring projects were supported and completed. Mapping these geniuses across our organization gave us a common language to talk about work, clarified why certain tasks energized some people while exhausting others, and helped us align responsibilities more intentionally. It also reinforced a truth at the heart of servant leadership: when people are empowered to operate from their strengths, both the individual and the organization flourish.

In the early days of the company, I poured countless nights and weekends into writing proposals. Many of them were for contracts we had little chance of winning, but I was convinced that sheer effort and determination could compensate for our lack of experience and positioning. My team, however, often tried to tell me otherwise. They cautioned that we were not ready, that the opportunities did not align with our strengths, or that chasing them would stretch us too thin. Instead of listening, I pushed ahead, expecting them to rally behind my vision. I mistook persistence for leadership and pressure for inspiration. The result was predictable: repeated rejection from proposal reviewers and growing frustration within my own team. I thought I was leading us forward, but in truth, I was eroding trust by ignoring the very people whose insight we needed most.

Moving through failure toward a more genuine implementation of servant leadership was transformative. It required a profound reevaluation of my actions and their impact on the team's dynamics. By adopting a coaching mindset, asking guiding questions, and stepping back to let the team lead their initiatives, I fostered a culture of trust, creativity, and empowerment. This transition was not instantaneous but a deliberate process of growth and adaptation, underscored by the willingness to learn from mistakes and embrace vulnerability.

Identifying the needs of the team begins with curiosity and presence. I learned that instead of assuming what people needed, I had to ask and then listen. Simple, consistent questions such as "What's getting in your way right now?", "What work energizes you most?" or "What support would make you more effective?" opened doors to conversations that revealed far more than performance metrics ever could.

Observation also played a role: noticing who leaned in during brainstorming sessions, who stayed quiet in meetings but thrived one-on-one, and who repeatedly volunteered for certain tasks gave me clues about strengths and struggles alike. Beyond individual conversations, creating anonymous surveys and feedback loops provided team members with a safe space to express concerns they might not voice directly. Over time, these practices helped me see patterns—areas where the team lacked resources, where morale was slipping, or where untapped potential was waiting. Identifying needs, I discovered, is less about conducting a single assessment and more about developing an ongoing posture of attentiveness, empathy, and openness to feedback.

The essence of servant leadership is encapsulated in the transition from acknowledging personal failures to adopting a leadership style that genuinely serves the team's needs. This path taught me the importance of empowering team members to be autonomous, the value of learning from failure, and the profound impact of a leadership approach that prioritizes the development and well-being of others. Through this evolution, I learned that the most effective way to lead is by serving, listening, and enabling the success of others, which, in turn, leads to the collective success of the organization. This realization has not only reshaped my approach to leadership but also cultivated a more engaged, resilient, and innovative team, showcasing the power of servant leadership in action.

Cultivating a Culture of Trust

Moving toward a servant leadership approach highlighted the paramount importance of trust within our organization. Trust, the very bedrock of any meaningful relationship, had to be nurtured and prioritized at every turn, starting fundamentally with how we engaged every member of our team in decision-making processes, far beyond just our hiring practices.

My personal journey to adopting servant leadership was marked by a pivotal realization regarding our approach to inclusivity and trust-building within the organization. Initially, decision-making, especially in critical areas like hiring, was confined to the leadership echelons. This method, although efficient from a managerial perspective, inadvertently created a chasm between leadership and the rest of the team. It was a system that unintentionally communicated a lack of faith in the insights and judgments of our broader team, including our administrative staff who interacted closely with candidates and had valuable insights to offer.

This realization hit hard. It became clear that by not involving the team in these decisions, we were not just overlooking potentially valuable input but were actively eroding the trust that is essential for a cohesive and motivated workforce. The administrative staff, despite their frontline interactions and contributions to the organization's daily operations, were never asked for their input on candidates—a glaring oversight, given their unique perspectives and the impact these new hires would have on their work life.

The adoption of servant leadership principles, mentioned at the end of Chapter 1, prompted a thorough reevaluation of our approach across the board. It wasn't just about improving our hiring practices but about instilling a culture of trust from the ground up, touching every aspect of our organization. We began to extend the principles of inclusivity, transparency, and mutual respect throughout all levels of decision-making, not just when bringing new members into our fold.

This meant opening up channels for feedback, encouraging open dialogues about company decisions, and involving team members in strategic discussions that would have once been reserved for leadership alone. These channels took many forms: semiannual town halls where anyone could raise questions directly, anonymous pulse surveys to surface concerns that might otherwise remain hidden, cross-functional working groups that brought together voices from different levels of the company, and an open-door office policy where leaders committed time simply to listen. Each of these practices reinforced the message that every perspective mattered and that decision-making was no longer confined to the top.

As Stephen R. Covey famously said, "Trust is the glue of life. It's the most essential ingredient in effective communication. It's the foundational principle that holds all relationships." This quote perfectly encapsulates the essence of our transformation. By embedding trust at the core of our operations, we sought to mend the gaps and build a stronger, more unified organization.

The transition to a more inclusive and trust-based culture had a profound impact. By demonstrating trust in our team members' judgments and valuing their contributions, we not only empowered them but also fostered a deeper sense of belonging and investment in the organization's success. This wasn't just about making better decisions through collective insight; it was about building an organizational culture where trust, respect, and mutual support were the norms.

Our administrative staff, once on the periphery of these critical decision-making processes, now felt more valued and integral to the organization's direction. One office manager told me after a few weeks on the job, "For the first time, I feel like I'm not just keeping things running; I'm helping shape where we're going." He had quickly developed the ability to anticipate several steps ahead, offering support that freed me to focus on higher-level work. That sense of being trusted and included gave him pride and motivation, and it was echoed by others on the team who said they finally felt their perspective mattered. This inclusivity bolstered morale and fostered a sense of ownership across all levels of the team, enhancing our overall cohesion and effectiveness.

Cultivating a culture of trust through servant leadership taught us invaluable lessons about the power of inclusivity and the importance of every team member's voice. By broadening the scope of involvement in decision-making and demonstrating genuine trust in our team's capabilities and insights, we not only strengthened our internal bonds but also set a foundation for a more resilient, motivated, and united organization. This evolution, though challenging, underscored the critical role of trust in achieving true servant leadership and the profound impact it can have on an organization's culture and success.

Reorienting Leadership Practices

The transition towards servant leadership was marked by a series of revelations and adjustments born out of real-world experiences. As I embarked on this path, founding my own business with the belief that my intelligence and capability to "do everything" would naturally translate into effective leadership, I quickly encountered the limitations of this approach.

My initial leadership style was predicated on the assumption that being smart and capable meant I could handle all aspects of the business single-handedly. This mindset, however, was flawed and led to a critical misstep: *If I could do everything myself, what was the role of my team?* Operating under this paradigm meant that all strategic thinking and planning remained with me, relegating my team to mere executors of tasks. This approach not only stifled creativity and initiative but also inadvertently sent a message that I did not trust their competence or value their contributions. The realization that my actions could be perceived as demeaning or dismissive was a sobering moment. It was akin to indirectly questioning their intelligence and worth, a notion that deeply troubled me.

Acknowledging the need for change, I began to reorient my leadership approach towards one that truly embraced the principles of servant leadership. This meant a deliberate shift from being the sole decision-maker to becoming a facilitator of success. I started by actively listening to my team, genuinely seeking to understand their aspirations, strengths, and the challenges they faced. This process involved redefining my role to be more accessible and supportive, focusing on enabling my team's personal and professional growth.

The shift in my leadership style was guided by three pivotal questions that helped me delegate more effectively and empower my team:

1. *Who is best suited to take on this task?* This question helped identify the right person for each task based on their skills and strengths, rather than arbitrarily assigning tasks.
2. *Do they have a genuine interest in this area?* Aligning tasks with team members' interests ensured that they were more engaged and motivated to deliver their best.
3. *Can they make a significant impact?* By ensuring that each task had the potential for meaningful impact, team members felt their work was valuable and recognized.

Adopting this new approach revolutionized my leadership practice. I moved from dictating tasks to empowering my team members to take ownership of projects that aligned with their strengths and interests. This not only motivated them but also fostered a sense of trust and respect within the team. By entrusting them with complete projects, rather than piecemeal tasks, I communicated my confidence in their abilities and my appreciation for their unique contributions to our collective success.

The reorientation of our leadership practices to prioritize listening, understanding, and facilitating marked a significant turning point. It cultivated an environment where team members felt valued, empowered, and motivated to innovate and take initiative. This shift towards servant leadership not only enhanced our team dynamics but also drove our business forward, demonstrating the profound impact of leadership that is rooted in service, trust, and empowerment.

Overcoming Challenges

Fully integrating servant leadership principles within our organization was a testament to both the resilience required to enact meaningful change and the profound impact such a transformation can have on a company's culture. My personal commitment to servant leadership was unwavering; I was all in. My business partner, too, embraced this new direction with open arms. However, as we began to cascade these principles down the organization, particularly to team members who had been with us before the shift, we encountered unexpected resistance.

The crux of the problem became apparent: the existing second layer of management was not on board with the shift towards servant leadership. Despite our best efforts to communicate the value and principles of this leadership approach, a significant disconnect remained. These managers, accustomed to traditional hierarchical structures and methods of control, found it difficult to adapt to a culture that prioritized empowerment, active listening, and supporting team members over directing them. This misalignment created a barrier to fully realizing the servant leadership culture we envisioned.

This resistance was a major hurdle. It highlighted a critical oversight in our approach to implementing servant leadership: assuming that a top-down directive would be sufficient to inspire change throughout the organization. Our initial strategy failed to account for the deeply ingrained habits and beliefs held by some of our team leaders, who were pivotal in shaping the day-to-day culture of our teams.

Recognizing that the path forward required more than just advocacy for servant leadership, we took decisive action. We reevaluated our leadership team, leading to the difficult decision to replace those second-tier managers who could not or would not embrace the servant leadership model. This process was challenging and required a level of patience and determination to see it through. Moreover, we flattened the organization's structure, aiming to reduce the layers of hierarchy that had perpetuated the old leadership paradigms.

This reorganization was not merely about changing personnel but was a strategic move to cultivate a breeding ground for servant leadership principles to flourish. By carefully selecting leaders who not only understood but lived these values, we began to see a positive evolution in the organizational culture.

As we solidified this new leadership framework, the principles of servant leadership began to permeate every level of the organization. This was not just an internal win; the impact extended beyond our immediate team to influence how we interacted with clients and vendors. By living the values of servant leadership, we started to see a positive ripple effect, fostering a culture of trust, collaboration, and mutual respect that extended to our external partnerships.

The propagation of servant leadership principles beyond our organizational boundaries became a testament to the power of this approach. It underscored the idea that by embodying these values, we could not only enhance our internal dynamics but also elevate our engagements with clients and vendors, creating a broader ecosystem of mutual support and empowerment.

The road to fully embracing servant leadership was long and fraught with challenges. However, each step, each decision to stay true to these principles, proved invaluable. The evolution of our organizational culture, marked by the adoption of servant leadership at all levels, demonstrated the profound impact of leading by serving. It reaffirmed our belief that the most effective way to inspire change and drive success is by fostering an environment where every individual feels valued, empowered, and motivated to contribute to a shared vision. This journey, though arduous, was a testament to the enduring power of servant leadership to transform not just an organization but its wider community of stakeholders.

Measuring Success

The transition to servant leadership within our organization was not just a shift in our management philosophy; it was a process that reshaped our entire operational ethos. The impact was profound, with measurable outcomes that far exceeded our initial expectations. Reflecting on this experience, the metrics of success were both quantitative and qualitative, painting a comprehensive picture of the growth and revitalization of our organizational culture.

One of the most striking indicators of success was the dramatic improvement in our annual team member retention rate, which skyrocketed from 54% to an astounding 97%. This leap was not merely a statistic but a testament to the profound sense of belonging, value, and satisfaction that team members felt within the newly cultivated servant leadership environment. The sense of community, mutual respect, and shared purpose fostered by servant leadership played a pivotal role in this achievement, transforming our organization into a place where people not only wanted to work but were also eager to contribute and grow.

Equally remarkable was our organization's growth, which we experienced fivefold. This growth was a direct result of the empowerment and autonomy that servant leadership principles encouraged among our team members. By shifting the focus from top-down directives to fostering an environment where ideas, creativity, and innovation were nurtured, we unlocked the potential of our team in ways we had never before imagined. This empowerment led to a surge in productivity and efficiency, driving our organization forward at an unprecedented pace.

One of the ways we harnessed this creativity was through our Idea Pitch program, a monthly "Shark Tank"-style event with four 15-minute slots for team members to present their ideas directly to leadership. What made the program powerful wasn't just the format, but the follow-through: approved ideas were greenlit for implementation on the spot. I still remember one pitch from a relatively new team member who suggested a streamlined onboarding checklist that combined compliance steps with cultural touchpoints. It seemed simple at first, but when we implemented it, the effect was dramatic—new hires integrated faster and felt more connected, and managers saved hours each week. Stories like this multiplied month after month, showing us that innovation doesn't only come from the top; it comes from creating a system where everyone has permission to contribute.

The number of ideas being generated by team members for business or organizational improvements was another area where we saw a dramatic change. From a baseline of zero, we moved to an environment where each team member contributed an average of 2-3 creative solutions. This explosion of creativity and innovation clearly indicated that our team members felt supported and valued, understanding that their ideas were not just welcomed but essential to our collective success.

Another significant shift was in how team members approached their work. The culture of autonomy fostered by servant leadership led to team members taking on tasks and responsibilities without the need for explicit permission. This shift represented a move away from a permission-based work culture to one of trust and empowerment, where the initiative was not just encouraged but became the norm. The amount of activity and engagement within the team increased tremendously, reflecting a vibrant and dynamic work environment.

One of the most impactful changes was the shift in focus for our leaders. With the principles of servant leadership firmly in place, leaders were freed from the minutiae of mission-centric tasks, allowing them to concentrate on the broader vision of the organization. This shift enabled strategic thinking, long-term planning, and a focus on sustainability and growth, further propelling our organization toward its goals.

The change to servant leadership within our organization was marked by significant challenges, but the outcomes speak volumes about the efficacy of this approach. The improvements in retention rates, organizational growth, innovation, autonomy, and strategic focus were not just metrics of success but markers of a profound cultural shift. They highlighted the power of servant leadership not only to enhance operational efficiency but also to create an organizational culture that is vibrant, inclusive, and forward-thinking. This experience, rooted in my personal commitment to servant leadership, underscored the undeniable impact that a leadership style focused on serving and empowering others can have on every aspect of an organization.

A Journey of Continuous Learning

Embarking on the path to servant leadership was characterized by continuous learning, adaptation, and an unwavering commitment to growth. Our initial steps towards embodying the principles of servant leadership within our organization set the foundation for a dynamic culture shift. However, as we aligned more closely with these principles, it became evident that there is no definitive endpoint. Instead, it is a perpetual process of evolution, requiring constant nurturing to keep the momentum alive and the culture vibrant.

To sustain the transformation and keep the spirit of servant leadership alive within our organization, we recognized the need to continually introduce new initiatives and learning opportunities. This led us to implement several key programs aimed at fostering innovation, leadership development, and deeper engagement across all levels of the organization. Most notably, our idea pitch program and our book club bring the team together to explore works on leadership, strategy, and personal growth. These initiatives, along with others, have created an environment where continuous learning, creativity, and collaboration are not just encouraged but embedded in our culture. It also spurred the following:

Idea Generation Workshops: To harness the collective creativity and insights of our team members, we introduced workshops focused on generating new ideas for business improvement, product innovation, and operational efficiency. These sessions serve as a platform for every voice to be heard and every suggestion to be valued, reinforcing the servant leadership tenet of empowering others.

80/20 Transformation: Inspired by the Pareto Principle, we embarked on an 80/20 transformation initiative, aiming to identify and focus on the 20% of efforts that yield 80% of our results. This approach not only encourages efficiency and strategic thinking but also integrates the application of three pivotal questions that reshaped my approach to delegation and empowerment.

Defining 'Who's' in Our Team: Understanding that each team member brings unique strengths and aspirations to the table, we made a concerted effort to define the 'Who's' within our organization. This involved mapping out roles based on individual strengths, passions, and potential for impact, thereby ensuring that everyone is positioned to contribute in the most meaningful way.

Leadership Retreat Workshops: Recognizing the importance of ongoing leadership development, we implemented various workshops designed to refine and expand our leadership skills. These sessions cover a range of topics, from communication and emotional intelligence to strategic planning and conflict resolution, ensuring our leaders are well-equipped to support and guide their teams effectively.

Client Alignment with Our Principles: To extend the reach of our servant leadership culture beyond our organization, we began intentionally sharing our principles with our clients. By openly communicating our leadership philosophy and practices, we foster shared understanding, build trust, and strengthen our partnerships through mutual respect and collaboration.

Communication Styles Training: Understanding that effective communication is the backbone of successful leadership and teamwork, we introduced training sessions focused on identifying and adapting to various communication styles. This initiative helps ensure that our interactions are as effective and empathetic as possible, further enhancing team cohesion and collaboration.

The Path Forward

As we continue on this path of continuous learning and adaptation, our commitment to the principles of servant leadership remains steadfast. We are dedicated to refining our approach, drawing on our experiences, and embracing new strategies to cultivate a leadership style that consistently brings out the best in our team members. It is an ongoing process, and with each step, we deepen our understanding, expand our capabilities, and reinforce our commitment to a culture of service, empowerment, and mutual growth.

In the chapters that follow, we will delve into the practical applications of servant leadership across various organizational contexts. I aim to provide leaders with actionable insights and strategies for implementing this approach within their teams and organizations, sharing the lessons I've learned and the successes achieved. This is not just a story of change; it is a blueprint for building a future where servant leadership is the norm, fostering environments where innovation, collaboration, and shared success flourish. But trust doesn't stop at the office door. Building a foundation of servant leadership within our team was only the first step. The next challenge was just as important: how could we extend that same culture of trust to our clients, partners, and the broader network within which we worked? The lessons we had learned internally would soon be tested externally, as we discovered what it meant to practice trust-based leadership in every relationship, not just inside the company.

CHAPTER 3

Cultivating Trust-Based Relationships Beyond the Organization

S everal years into our journey, I sat across the table from a senior executive at a large public organization—one of our most important clients. We had worked with them for months, and by all appearances, the project was going well. Our team was delivering on deadlines, producing quality work, and building rapport with staff. But in the middle of what I assumed would be a routine check-in, the executive leaned back in his chair and said something that stopped me cold: *"We trust your people, but we don't always understand how you make decisions."*

At first, I wanted to defend us. We were working hard, weren't we? But as I thought about it, I realized he was right. Inside our company, we had worked diligently to build a culture of transparency and trust. Everyone could see how decisions were made and understood why. Yet with this client, our communication often stopped at deliverables. We were giving them the "what," but not the "why" behind it. They trusted our competence but felt disconnected from our process.

That conversation was a turning point. It made me realize that the principles of servant leadership and trust-based culture couldn't stay within our own four walls. If our clients and partners didn't feel the same level of openness and integrity, we were leaving trust unfinished. It wasn't enough to serve our team; we had to serve our clients with the same mindset, inviting them into the process, listening to their concerns, and being as transparent with them as we were with each other.

Our commitment to trust-based leadership extended beyond internal dynamics to encompass all interactions with clients, prospective clients, and partners. We adopted a philosophy of transparency, integrity, and mutual support, actively listening to and understanding the needs of those we worked with, thereby building strong, trustful relationships that set new standards for reliability and excellence.

Extending the Philosophy of Trust: Building Trust Through Personal Relationships

Our efforts to extend the philosophy of trust beyond our organizational boundaries taught us a crucial lesson: building trust with external stakeholders involves more than just business discussions; it requires developing personal relationships with them. Understanding what motivates our partners and what is important to them became a pivotal aspect of our approach.

In the early days of our partnership with the company for which we became a subcontractor, we recognized that establishing trust was not going to be instantaneous. It required effort, understanding, and a genuine interest in the leadership and operational ethos of our teaming partner. This realization led us to engage more deeply with their team, not only in professional settings but also in personal and social contexts.

We invested time in attending their social events, participating in informal breakfasts, lunches, and dinners. These gatherings provided invaluable insights into the personalities, values, and priorities that drove the leadership and operational strategies of our partner. Through these interactions, we learned about the importance of aligning our actions with what mattered most to them, ensuring that our services and interactions supported their broader goals and values.

This approach to building trust is echoed in Patrick Lencioni's book *Getting Naked,* where he advocates for vulnerability in professional services. Lencioni suggests that the fear of losing business prevents providers from being vulnerable and transparent with clients, yet it is this very vulnerability that fosters trust and loyalty. By adopting a 'naked' approach, where we were open about our capabilities, attentive to their needs, and willing to show our dedication beyond contractual obligations, we demonstrated a level of vulnerability that deepened our relationship with the partner.

Our commitment to understanding the motivations and operations of our partners' leadership went beyond mere professional courtesy; it was a strategic and heartfelt effort to build a partnership based on trust, respect, and mutual understanding. We realized that trust is not built solely through delivering excellent work; it is also cultivated by showing genuine interest in the people with whom we work, understanding their challenges, and celebrating their successes as if they were our own.

This highlighted a fundamental truth: it is far more valuable to create a few quality, trust-based relationships than to spread oneself thin across many superficial connections. The depth of a few meaningful partnerships can offer more sustained value and impact than superficially knowing a wide array of people or companies. This principle guided us to prioritize depth over breadth in our relationships, understanding that the strength of our business ties would not come from the quantity of our connections but from the quality of trust and mutual respect we nurtured within them.

The results of this approach were profound. We maintained a strong and productive partnership with the company for 10 years, a testament to the strength and mutual respect for the relationship we had built. Even as we navigated the complexities of business, our commitment to understanding and meeting their needs helped us establish a partnership that was resilient, mutually beneficial, and rewarding.

The journey with this partner, which lasted until their company was acquired, serves as a powerful example of how extending the philosophy of trust beyond the confines of our organization can lead to long-lasting and meaningful business relationships. It taught us that by prioritizing transparency, integrity, and mutual support, and by focusing on creating value for all involved, we could build partnerships that withstand the test of time and change. This experience has been a cornerstone in our approach to cultivating trust-based relationships, not just within our organization but with all external stakeholders.

This deepened relationship paid dividends not just in the form of a decade-long partnership but also in the lessons we learned about the importance of personal connections in business. We came to understand that trust-based leadership is as much about the heart as it is about the mind. Our partnership with this client grew not only through delivering results but also through the time we spent together outside of formal meetings—sharing meals after long project days, attending events they cared about, and getting to know their families and personal interests. These moments of genuine connection built familiarity and goodwill that no contract could replicate.

By integrating ourselves into the fabric of our partners' social and professional lives, we were able to build a bond that was resilient, respectful, and mutually beneficial. The foundation of any enduring business relationship is not just the quality of work provided but also the depth of the personal connections formed, underscoring the importance of prioritizing a few quality, trust-based relationships over numerous superficial ones.

Transparency with Clients and Partners: A Journey from Overselling to Authenticity

Moving towards transparency with clients and partners began with a stark realization about the pitfalls of overselling our capabilities. Like many ambitious companies, we aimed to be the best in our field. However, in our eagerness to impress clients and partners, we often found ourselves discussing services and capabilities that were beyond our proven experience. This attempt to be everything to everyone soon revealed its flaws.

As a small business, it didn't take long for others to see through our overstated capabilities. We lacked the personnel and expertise to deliver on all the services we had ambitiously promised. Ignoring this reality led to a costly cycle of trying to build our services "on the fly" to deliver them. This approach, although it might sound like agility, resulted in numerous errors, re-dos, and an unsustainable business model.

The shift came when we recognized the need to stop chasing every shiny object and instead focus on our core strengths. This required a painful but necessary shift towards transparency with our clients and partners. We began to communicate openly about our real capabilities, our processes, and the realistic expectations of what we could deliver. This transition was initially challenging, as it meant admitting our limitations and redefining our value proposition.

However, the dividends of honesty were immense. Clients and partners began to recognize and appreciate our authenticity. They saw that there was no fluff in our promises; what we offered was genuine, achievable, and backed by a commitment to quality. This transparency laid the groundwork for a higher degree of trust and collaboration.

Transparency is indeed the cornerstone of trust. By embracing open communication about our capabilities, timelines, and the challenges we faced, we aligned more closely with our clients and partners. This alignment reduced misunderstandings and fostered a sense of security and mutual respect. It showed that we were not only invested in our success, but in the success of our partners and clients, thus driving deeper, more meaningful relationships.

Integrity in Every Interaction: Upholding Our Core Values

Integrity forms the backbone of trust-based leadership, guiding us through every interaction, both internally and with external stakeholders. It's about more than just honesty; it's about consistently aligning our actions with our moral and ethical principles, regardless of the circumstances. This unwavering commitment to integrity ensures that every decision we make not only benefits our organization but is also fair and respectful towards our clients and partners. By embodying these values, we foster a culture of reliability and trust that encourages all stakeholders to engage with us more deeply.

However, maintaining this integrity is not without its challenges, especially in the consulting industry, where our employees often work closely with client teams. It's an environment ripe for potential conflict, where misunderstandings or disagreements can quickly escalate. In such situations, it's all too easy for consultants, who are often seen as temporary fixtures, to be blamed for errors or miscommunications. Succumbing to this blame game, however, is not in our nature. It contradicts the very essence of the culture we strive to build, both within our organization and in our engagements with clients.

A recent incident put our commitment to integrity to the test. One of our employees, while engaged in a project, spoke an uncomfortable truth to a member of the client's organization. In response, the client requested that we remove this employee from the support team. Complying with this request would have been the easier path, avoiding immediate conflict and potentially preserving the business relationship in the short term. However, it would also have represented a significant breach of our values, undermining the trust we place in our team members and compromising our integrity.

Faced with this dilemma, we chose to stand behind our team member. We engaged in a frank discussion with our client, explaining our values of honesty, transparency, and integrity. It was not about defiance but about affirming the principles that guide our actions and decisions. We clarified that while we are committed to our clients' success, we cannot do so at the expense of our core values or the trust and respect we have for our employees.

This decision to uphold our values above expediency was a moment of truth for our organization. It reaffirmed to our team that we are an organization that lives by its principles, even when it's challenging. It also sent a powerful message to our client and other stakeholders about what we stand for.

To our relief and satisfaction, the client ultimately respected our stance. They agreed to keep our team member on the project, and through this experience, began to reflect the values of integrity and honesty that we champion. This incident not only strengthened our relationship with the client but also reinforced our reputation as a trustworthy and principled partner.

Integrity in every interaction is not just a moral imperative; it's a strategic advantage. It builds a foundation of trust that can withstand the inevitable challenges and conflicts that arise in any business relationship. By consistently demonstrating integrity, we not only ensure that our organization acts in a fair and respectful manner but also encourage our clients and partners to invest their trust in us. This commitment to integrity, even in the face of potential loss, is what differentiates us in a competitive market and cements our reputation as a reliable and ethical leader.

Mutual Support as a Partnership Philosophy: Beyond Business Boundaries

Mutual support forms the cornerstone of any lasting relationship, transcending the traditional boundaries of business transactions and touching upon the very essence of human connection and empathy. This philosophy of mutual support not only defines our internal culture but extends how we interact with external stakeholders, including clients and partners. It's about proactively anticipating and addressing the needs of others and demonstrating a commitment to their well-being that goes beyond contractual obligations.

Our commitment to this philosophy was put to the test in a challenging situation involving one of our team members who went through a serious mental health crisis. This crisis had a profound impact on his performance, leading to noticeable incoherence in his work environment. The situation was visible to both our clients and other team members, signaling deep underlying issues that needed immediate attention.

Given the circumstances, we made the difficult decision to remove the team member from the project and, eventually, ask him to leave the company. However, this did not mark the end of our responsibility towards him. True to our philosophy of mutual support, we continued to communicate with him beyond his employment with our company.

Initially, this communication was fraught with tension and contention, marked by threats that stemmed from his mental health condition. Despite these challenges, we felt a deep sense of duty to assist him through this tumultuous period.

As a leader, I devoted a significant amount of my time to this issue, driven by the conviction that it was the right thing to do. Our efforts were not limited to severing ties but extended to actively supporting him on the road to recovery and reintegration, going beyond the call of duty. We facilitated his reunion with his family, from whom he had been estranged for many years. Moreover, we played a pivotal role in helping him re-enter the workforce, leveraging our network to secure a position for him within our client organization.

This approach was not born out of obligation but from a genuine desire to uphold our values of mutual support and empathy. It underscored the belief that our responsibility toward our team members extends beyond their tenure with the company, embracing a more holistic view of their well-being.

Extending Support in Times of Illness

Another profound example of our commitment to mutual support was when we worked with a client lead who became terminally ill. Faced with this heart-wrenching situation, our team exemplified the essence of our partnership philosophy, extending their support far beyond the usual scope of their duties.

Our team members took it upon themselves to cover all of the lead's tasks and responsibilities, managing day-to-day interactions and assignments to alleviate the client's physical and mental burden. This endeavor was not taken lightly; it required a significant emotional and professional investment from our team. However, guided by our belief in doing the right thing, we went above and beyond to help ease the pain of someone in need.

This commitment to supporting our client during such a vulnerable time not only helped maintain the project's momentum but also strengthened the bond between our organizations. It was a clear demonstration that our philosophy of mutual support transcends business transactions, touching the lives of individuals in meaningful and compassionate ways.

Mutual support, as a partnership philosophy, is about recognizing that the strength of our relationships, both internal and external, is measured not just by our successes, but by how we support each other through challenges. These instances of providing support during times of personal crisis underscore our commitment to a culture of compassion and empathy. By acting on this philosophy, we build not only professionally rewarding relationships but also deeply human connections, enriching our collective experience beyond the confines of business.

Actively Listening and Understanding Needs: The Foundation of Trust-Based Relationships

The ability to actively listen and understand the needs of clients and partners forms the bedrock of enduring relationships and trust-based leadership. Active listening goes beyond the simple act of hearing words; it involves engaging with and processing the needs, concerns, and feedback of our stakeholders with a level of empathy and attention that transcends conventional communication.

Embracing active listening in today's world requires a true dedication that cannot be understated. The task is made increasingly difficult by the myriad distractions that pervade our society, from the constant pings of technology to the noise of our surroundings. To actively listen is to consciously silence these distractions, to prioritize the person in front of us over the incessant demands for our attention that characterize modern life. This level of attentiveness signals to clients and partners that their voice is not only heard but deeply valued. It's about listening to understand, not just to respond. Through this practice, we convey a genuine interest in their perspectives, which is crucial for fostering a sense of respect and appreciation. Achieving this state of focused listening is challenging; it requires a deliberate effort to be present, proof of the listener's commitment to the relationship.

Empathy is at the heart of active listening. It involves putting ourselves in our stakeholders' shoes, understanding their situation, and feeling what they feel. However, empathy alone is not enough; it must be coupled with action. Active listening informs our responses and actions, ensuring they are tailored to address the specific needs and concerns of our clients and partners. This responsiveness demonstrates our commitment to their satisfaction and well-being, reinforcing the trust they place in us.

Listening to the needs of our clients is crucial to delivering the right solution. Missing the mark not only fails to address the client's issue but can also lead to significant errors. Our clients seek our help because they need it; our job is to be one hundred percent focused on providing that help. This commitment to understanding and meeting their needs allows us to tailor our services in a way that truly benefits them, enhancing satisfaction and cementing trust.

My experience in mastering active listening and truly understanding the needs around me began as a quest to assert my intelligence and capability in the professional sphere. I prepared meticulously for meetings and presentations, aiming to project the best version of myself. My presentations were polished and my knowledge was showcased. However, this approach had unintended consequences. It positioned me as the "know-it-all," inadvertently disempowering my colleagues. The message was inadvertently clear: Why bother contributing if he will always find a way to do it better?

This realization sparked a significant mental metamorphosis. I recognized the need to step back, to speak less, and to let others take the lead. Transitioning from being the perpetual leader to a collaborative team member was challenging. Moments still arise when my instinct is to take charge, but I've learned the importance of pausing and reminding myself to allow others the space to excel and contribute.

Integrating active listening into my leadership style underscored how deeply active listening and trust are intertwined. Trust and active listening are fundamental to each other; no one can truly trust without being listened to, and active listening forms the building block of trust. I've learned that my role is not to dominate but to facilitate an environment where every voice is heard, and every contribution is valued. This mutual trust has become a cornerstone of my leadership, enabling a culture where everyone feels empowered to contribute their best.

Combining my personal transformation with the practice of actively listening and understanding has reinforced the importance of this approach in building trust-based relationships. By prioritizing active listening in our interactions, we demonstrate a respect for our stakeholders that goes beyond mere business transactions. This approach not only enhances satisfaction and trust but also lays the groundwork for long-lasting, meaningful partnerships that can withstand the challenges of an ever-changing business landscape.

Through active listening, we affirm our dedication to the success and well-being of our clients and partners, reinforcing the foundation of trust upon which our relationships are built. I've learned that leadership is as much about listening and empowering others as it is about guiding and decision-making. In embracing this philosophy, we create a culture of mutual respect, shared goals, and collective success.

Setting New Standards for Reliability and Excellence

In our commitment to embodying trust-based leadership, we recognized early on that the essence of our endeavor stretched far beyond the confines of our organization. It was about fostering profound connections with our external stakeholders—clients, partners, and the broader community. This process taught us that adopting a philosophy of transparency, integrity, and mutual support, coupled with the unwavering commitment to actively listen and truly understand the needs of those we serve, would set us apart in a competitive landscape. These core principles not only enhanced our relationships but also established new benchmarks for what reliability and excellence could look like in our industry.

Several years ago, we embarked on a project with a new client, one that we were eager to impress by delivering unparalleled service. We boasted about the exceptional work we were doing and the significant improvements we believed we were making within their organization. However, it was soon brought to our attention that our perception was not entirely accurate. Despite our best intentions, we were unaware of the actual impact we were having.

Driven by a desire to genuinely understand our performance from the client's perspective, we initiated direct conversations with key individuals within their organization. It was through these discussions that we confronted a reality we had not anticipated: issues with the quality of our work and a concerning rate of turnover among our team members. This feedback was a stark departure from the narrative we had convinced ourselves was true.

This revelation marked a pivotal moment. It forced us to confront the truth about our performance and to question the efficacy of our approach. Rather than defending our position or dismissing the feedback, we chose to embrace it. We acknowledged our shortcomings to the client, committing to a path of continuous improvement and honest communication. This shift in approach was not easy, but it was necessary. It transformed our relationship with the client, moving us from a vendor to a trusted partner.

The changes we implemented were profound, affecting every level of our operations. We focused on improving the quality of our work, addressing the root causes of staff turnover, and ensuring that our actions aligned with our client's expectations and needs. By doing so, we not only improved our service delivery but also demonstrated our commitment to integrity and accountability.

Moving toward organizational improvement and excellence is grounded in the principle of honesty. Only by being honest about what is happening both internally and externally can we gather accurate data that forms the basis for meaningful improvement. Without a truthful understanding of our performance, we lack a solid foundation to build upon. This honesty extends beyond acknowledging our successes; it involves a willingness to confront our failures and the areas where we fall short.

The importance of trust in this process cannot be overstated, especially when it comes to business process improvement. Trust facilitates open and honest communication, ensuring that feedback is received and acted upon constructively. In an environment where trust prevails, team members feel secure in voicing concerns, sharing insights, and suggesting improvements without fear of reprisal. This culture of trust and transparency is essential for continuous process improvement, as it allows organizations to adapt, evolve, and maintain a competitive edge.

The outcome of our willingness to listen, adapt, and improve was extraordinary. Seventeen years later, that client remains with us, a testament to the strength and durability of the trust we have built together. The foundation of our relationship, cemented in mutual respect and honest communication, allowed us to set new standards for reliability and excellence within our industry.

Our experience with this client illustrates the power of trust-based leadership. By being transparent about our capabilities and limitations, by showing integrity in the face of challenges, and by providing unwavering support, we have fostered enduring relationships that transcend typical business transactions. These relationships are the pillars upon which our reputation for excellence is built.

The principles of trust-based leadership have guided us to not only improve our internal culture but also to redefine our interactions with clients and the broader community. This approach has enabled us to establish new benchmarks for reliability and excellence, distinguishing our organization in a competitive market. It has been both humbling and rewarding, teaching us that the most impactful strategy for lasting success lies in the strength of the trust we build with every stakeholder we serve.

Yet as we wrestled with these lessons, it became clear that trust could not be managed in fragments—internal trust here, client trust there. We needed a comprehensive framework to guide us across every relationship, both within and outside the company. That realization gave birth to what we call Trust 360.

PART II Present:

Leading with Trust Today

Clarifying "Trust 360". Building Holistic Trust in All Organizational Relationships

I t's crucial to distinguish our use of "Trust 360" from any similar terms in other industries. Here, it represents a comprehensive approach to building trust in all organizational relationships— internally with team members and externally with clients and partners. This holistic view of trust underscores our belief in its foundational role in achieving organizational success and fostering a positive culture.

A Lesson Learned the Hard Way

Early in my career, I started a determined company with a clear ambition: to grow rapidly and establish itself as a leader in the industry. Our defining moment came when we landed a major client, a global organization that promised to be our springboard to success. It was an opportunity we knew could revolutionize our business. We believed that if we could deliver exceptional results for this client, it would open the doors to more significant opportunities. It felt like the golden ticket we'd been striving for, and we committed ourselves fully to making it a success.

In our zeal to impress, we embraced the commonly held belief that "the client is everything," subordinating all other priorities to meet this client's demands. We pushed our team members to the limit, sending them across the country and around the world at a moment's notice. There were weekends when they had just 24 to 48 hours at home before embarking on the next assignment. We spared no effort and left no opportunity unattended, ensuring that we captured as much work as possible, even when it meant overextending our teams.

Our partner companies felt the pressure, too. As we sought to secure a larger share of the work, collaboration began to shift toward competition. Trust, once the foundation of these relationships, started to erode. The drive to serve our client at all costs led us to neglect our partners' contributions, creating tension and weakening alliances. As the months turned into years, the strain became unbearable. Team members, overwhelmed by constant travel and unrealistic expectations, began to leave. Their personal lives were strained, their families were affected, and eventually, burnout set in. The turnover was significant, resulting in the loss of invaluable knowledge and experience.

As the quality of our work declined, the client began to notice. Despite all our sacrifices, things weren't as smooth or memorable as we had hoped. The project concluded after nearly six years, but there were no follow-up contracts. The opportunity we had worked so hard for didn't yield the future business we expected. The lessons we learned were harsh but necessary: focusing solely on one client at the expense of all others, including employees, partners, and even the broader community, had compromised the foundation of our success.

This experience forced us to confront a flawed mindset that is pervasive in the business world: the notion that "the customer is king" and must be prioritized above all else. While these sayings are often touted in business schools and boardrooms, real-world experience shows that they are misguided. Sustainable success depends on building trust not just with clients but across all organizational relationships.

This realization led to the development of what we call Trust 360. It's crucial to distinguish our use of the term from any similar phrases in other industries. Here, Trust 360 represents a comprehensive approach to cultivating trust with every stakeholder—internally with team members, externally with clients, with partners, and with the broader community. This holistic view underscores our belief that trust is the foundation of organizational success and the anchor of a positive culture.

The Birth of Trust 360

Trust 360 emerged from a pivotal realization: sustainable success in business is not achieved by focusing solely on clients, but by building strong, mutually beneficial relationships with all stakeholders. The concept was born from hard-earned lessons about the importance of balancing trust across the organization. Trust 360 shifts the focus from prioritizing a single relationship to embracing a holistic view of trust that includes employees, partners, clients, and the community. This balanced approach recognizes that every stakeholder is interconnected, and when trust is nurtured equally among them, organizations can create a harmonious, resilient ecosystem that drives long-term growth.

Trust 360 is not a one-size-fits-all solution. It's an adaptable framework that organizations must tailor to their specific needs and culture. It emphasizes the idea that trust is foundational. It's not just a strategy or an initiative, but a core value that permeates every action, decision, and interaction. In the sections that follow, we'll dive deeper into how Trust 360 applies to each key stakeholder group and explore the practical strategies and real-world examples that demonstrate its effectiveness.

Trust with Employees

Employees are the heart and soul of any organization. Their well-being, motivation, and satisfaction have a direct impact on productivity, innovation, and retention. When employees feel trusted and valued, they become more engaged, proactive, and committed to the organization's mission. Building trust with employees goes beyond just providing clear instructions or managing day-to-day tasks—it requires a genuine investment in their personal and professional development, a commitment to transparent communication, and respect for their individual needs and well-being. Trust is not simply a managerial tool but a fundamental value that should be ingrained in the company's culture. This approach not only benefits employees but also enhances organizational performance. Employees who feel genuinely connected and appreciated tend to perform better and contribute more meaningfully to the company's success.

Open communication is the foundation of any trusting relationship, especially in the workplace. Employees want to feel included and informed about where the company is heading, what challenges it faces, and how their work contributes to its overall success. Establishing a culture of open communication involves more than simply relaying information; it requires a commitment to regular, transparent, and meaningful dialogue that keeps employees engaged and aligned with the company's goals.

Frequent updates play a vital role in building trust through communication. Sharing regular updates about company performance, ongoing projects, and strategic goals helps employees feel connected to the bigger picture. Many companies host monthly townhall meetings or virtual team gatherings where leaders provide a comprehensive update on the organization's progress, recent achievements, and strategic shifts. These sessions often feature a Q&A segment where employees can raise questions and express concerns, creating a two-way dialogue that fosters a sense of inclusion. For example, a manufacturing company might use these meetings to discuss quarterly performance, outlining how the efforts of different teams contributed to key outcomes and how upcoming initiatives align with broader company objectives. This level of transparency helps employees understand how their work fits into the larger vision, making them feel more integral to the organization's success.

Two-way feedback is equally important in fostering open communication. Employees should feel comfortable sharing their ideas, concerns, and suggestions, knowing that their voices will be heard and respected. This culture of feedback can be developed through regular one-on-one meetings between employees and managers, as well as through anonymous feedback channels, such as pulse surveys or suggestion boxes. For instance, a healthcare organization implemented quarterly anonymous surveys to gauge employee morale, identify workload concerns, and solicit feedback on company policies. Leadership then reviewed the feedback, discussed the findings openly in all-hands meetings, and outlined steps to address the key issues. This approach not only built trust but also demonstrated that employee feedback leads to tangible change, reinforcing the belief that every voice matters.

Transparency in decision-making is another element of open communication. When decisions are made—especially those that affect employees directly, such as policy changes, restructuring, or strategy shifts—leaders should communicate the "why" behind the decisions, not just the "what." For example, a financial services company might introduce a series of "strategy sessions" where executives explain the rationale behind major decisions, such as a restructuring of teams or the launch of a new service line. By providing context and addressing questions openly, employees gain a clearer understanding of the decision-making process, which helps align their efforts with the company's strategic goals and builds a sense of trust and inclusion.

Empowerment in the workplace is about enabling employees to take ownership of their work, drive innovation, and grow professionally. When employees are empowered, they feel more in control of their roles, more engaged in their work, and more invested in the organization's success. Empowering employees means giving them not only the tools and support they need but also the autonomy to make decisions and pursue opportunities for growth.

Autonomy in roles is a fundamental aspect of empowerment. Employees who are trusted to make decisions within their roles feel a greater sense of ownership and accountability. A retail chain might empower its store managers to make localized pricing decisions based on market trends, allowing them to tailor promotions to customer needs. This level of decision-making authority demonstrates trust in employees' judgment and knowledge of their local markets, which can result in improved sales and stronger employee engagement. This shift from a micromanagement approach to a coaching mindset allows employees to find their path to success while feeling supported by leadership.

Professional development is another key component of empowerment. Organizations that invest in training and development opportunities signal to employees that their growth is valued and that the organization is committed to their long-term success. This investment can take many forms, including technical skills training, leadership development programs, and mentorship initiatives. A marketing agency might establish an internal digital academy, where employees can earn certifications in areas like SEO, social media management, or data analytics. Employees who complete the program can then lead projects related to their new skills, reinforcing the connection between professional growth and organizational success.

One of the most powerful ways to empower employees is to create opportunities for them to bring their ideas to life. At our organization, the *Idea Pitch* initiative was designed with this purpose in mind. Employees are encouraged to propose projects, products, or process improvements they are passionate about, with a clear path to implementation if approved. This initiative is open to everyone, regardless of role or tenure. Once an idea is approved, the employee receives the necessary resources, support, and autonomy to lead the project. Recently, an employee pitched an automated client onboarding system aimed at streamlining processes and reducing errors. The idea was greenlit, and the employee led a cross-functional team to develop and launch the system, supported by mentorship from senior leadership. This initiative not only fosters a culture of creativity and innovation but also demonstrates a tangible commitment to employee empowerment, building trust by showing that their insights are valued and impactful.

Respecting the Whole Person

Maintaining work-life balance is essential for employee well-being and a key factor in building trust. Employees need to know that their personal lives are respected and that their workloads are reasonable. When organizations prioritize work-life balance, they send a clear message that they care about employees' holistic well-being, which in turn strengthens trust and commitment.

Realistic expectations are crucial in promoting work-life balance. Organizations need to understand the capacity of each team member and plan projects accordingly, regularly assessing and adjusting workloads to prevent burnout. For example, a software company might hold weekly check-ins to review workload distribution among team members, ensuring that no one is overwhelmed and that tasks are allocated fairly. These regular assessments not only help maintain a manageable workload but also reinforce trust by demonstrating that employee well-being is a priority.

Flexibility is another critical aspect of work-life balance. Offering flexible work arrangements, such as remote work options, flexible hours, or hybrid models, allows employees to better balance personal commitments with professional responsibilities. For instance, a consulting firm introduced a hybrid work model where employees could work from home two days a week. This flexibility led to higher job satisfaction, reduced commuting stress, and improved productivity, as employees were able to manage their time more effectively.

Support for well-being goes beyond managing workloads and offering flexible hours—it also involves actively promoting mental and physical health. Organizations that implement wellness programs, offer mental health days, or provide access to employee assistance programs demonstrate a commitment to holistic employee care. For example, a healthcare company might introduce "mental wellness days," allowing employees to take two annual days off specifically to focus on mental health, without using personal leave. This initiative not only promotes well-being but also reinforces the message that the organization values employees' mental health as much as their productivity.

Example of Good Practice

The Legendary Employee Growth Opportunity (LEGO) Team Member Benefits policy at our organization exemplifies a strong commitment to employee trust through empowerment, open communication, and support for work-life balance. This policy ensures that internal employees have priority access to all new job opportunities before they are offered to external candidates. It reflects a deep commitment to personal growth and demonstrates that the organization values its existing talent.

This approach not only empowers employees by offering clear paths for career advancement but also fosters trust by making internal mobility a transparent process. For instance, if a new managerial role opens up, internal employees are encouraged to apply and are given first consideration. This provides employees with a sense of security and opportunity, reinforcing the idea that their professional growth is a priority for the organization.

The LEGO Team Member Benefits policy works in tandem with initiatives like the Idea Pitch, where employees are encouraged to propose and implement their own projects. Together, these programs not only drive innovation but also build trust by showing that employees' skills and ideas are valued. This comprehensive commitment aligns with the principles of Trust 360, integrating empowerment, transparent communication, and genuine support for employees' career aspirations.

Trust with Partners

Developing trust with companies you are partnering with can be a challenging endeavor. Often, partnerships are born out of necessity rather than a shared vision. The initial questions are always the same: *Why was this partnership created? Is it simply to fill a gap in capabilities, or is there potential for a deeper, long-term collaboration?* In many cases, the answer is ambiguous. If the relationship begins with a narrow purpose, like filling a gap in expertise or capacity, it can lead to uncertainty about the future once that gap is addressed. The lack of clarity can result in partners feeling expendable, leading to protective behavior rather than open collaboration.

Reflecting on the introductory story of this chapter, when we won a major project with partners, we assumed they simply needed us to fill a specific role. We believed that once they had learned to fill that gap themselves, they would discard us as if we had never existed. On the other hand, the partners actually wanted to retain us for our expertise in specific areas, but this intention was never communicated clearly. The ambiguous communication on both sides led to a defensive posture, with each party keeping up shields and using significant energy to protect their respective interests rather than collaborating openly. Over the years, communication remained a persistent issue, with both sides struggling to understand each other's true intentions.

Building trust in a partnership requires moving beyond transactional interactions and developing a relationship based on mutual respect, clear goals, and honest dialogue. To do this effectively, partnerships must be grounded in three essential components: aligned objectives, fair collaboration, and transparent communication.

Aligned objectives help partnerships to thrive. Both parties must establish clear, shared goals that benefit all involved. Without aligned objectives, partnerships can easily become transactional, with each side focusing only on what they need to gain rather than how both can succeed together. To build trust, partners must start by understanding each other's long-term goals and strategic vision. Aligning objectives ensures that both parties are working toward mutually beneficial outcomes and that there is a shared sense of purpose driving the collaboration.

When entering a new partnership, it is essential to define not only the immediate project goals but also broader outcomes that reflect a long-term commitment. For example, when a construction firm partners with an architectural design firm for a building project, they must align not just on project timelines and quality standards but also on how each partner's expertise will contribute to client satisfaction and future projects. By setting clear, mutually agreed-upon objectives, both sides know exactly what success looks like and how to contribute to it. Regular check-ins to review progress and adjust strategies as needed help maintain this alignment and foster trust.

Moreover, it is essential that both sides perceive the partnership as providing value. It should not be one-sided or solely about fulfilling a temporary need. For example, a tech company that partners with a marketing agency for a product launch must ensure that both sides benefit, whether through increased sales, brand awareness, or customer engagement. When both sides feel that they are gaining from the partnership, trust naturally grows, and the collaboration is more likely to produce innovative and effective solutions. Aligning on long-term value, rather than just short-term gains, helps partners feel more invested in each other's success.

Fair collaboration is about more than just dividing tasks equitably. It involves respecting each partner's strengths, recognizing their contributions, and distributing opportunities and resources in a way that ensures mutual benefit. Trust grows when partners feel that the relationship is balanced and that their expertise is acknowledged and valued. If one partner consistently dominates the collaboration or overlooks the other's contributions, resentment can build, undermining trust and damaging the partnership.

Equitable resource sharing is one way to ensure fair collaboration. This means distributing workloads, responsibilities, and rewards based on each partner's capacity and expertise. For instance, in a consulting partnership between a management firm and a data analytics company, roles might be clearly defined, with the management firm focusing on strategy and client relations while the analytics company handles technical insights. By recognizing and leveraging each other's strengths, both partners can maximize their contributions and feel a sense of mutual respect.

Sharing risks and rewards is another vital aspect of fair collaboration. In long-term partnerships, it is essential to create agreements where both parties benefit proportionately from the outcomes. For example, two companies working together on a joint venture might agree to share both profits and risks according to predetermined ratios. This ensures that neither partner feels disadvantaged, fostering trust and encouraging both sides to invest more in the partnership. Knowing that their efforts will be fairly rewarded, partners are more likely to engage fully and bring their best to the collaboration.

Addressing conflicts constructively is equally important for fair collaboration. Disagreements are inevitable in any partnership, whether over project scope, resource allocation, or other issues. However, how conflicts are handled can either strengthen or weaken trust. When conflicts arise, both sides should approach resolution with openness and a focus on finding mutually beneficial solutions. For instance, if one partner feels that the workload has become imbalanced, it's crucial to engage in a candid dialogue to reassess roles and responsibilities. By addressing issues transparently and respectfully, partners maintain trust and keep the relationship strong.

Transparent communication is the glue that holds partnerships together. Going beyond basic updates or formal reporting, it requires proactive, honest, and consistent communication that keeps partners informed and engaged. Transparency involves sharing not only successes but also challenges, demonstrating a commitment to collaboration and problem-solving rather than blame-shifting.

Structured meetings are a practical way to ensure transparent communication. Regular strategy sessions or progress reviews provide an opportunity to share updates, discuss challenges, and adjust plans as needed. For example, two companies in a joint venture might hold bi-weekly strategy meetings where they openly share data, review milestones, and address any roadblocks. These meetings should be more than just updates; they should encourage open dialogue, where partners can ask questions, raise concerns, and propose solutions. By making communication a two-way street, partners build a sense of mutual understanding and trust.

Being upfront about both positive developments and setbacks is critical for transparency. If a digital marketing agency partnering with a software developer encounters unexpected delays in campaign execution, it should communicate the issue promptly and suggest solutions. This honesty not only maintains trust but also demonstrates a commitment to overcoming challenges together, rather than shifting blame.

Clear and fair negotiation is another key aspect of transparent communication. From the beginning, partners should engage in honest discussions about terms, expectations, and deliverables. A logistics company partnering with a distribution firm for a regional expansion should outline the scope of services, resource commitments, and timelines in a straightforward manner to prevent misunderstandings later. Open and fair negotiation sets a positive tone for the partnership, reinforcing trust and establishing a cooperative spirit.

Consider a scenario where two companies, a manufacturing firm and a logistics provider, enter into a long-term collaboration to optimize supply chain efficiency. Initially, both partners hold a joint planning session to establish aligned objectives, such as reducing lead times by 20% and cutting logistics costs by 15% within the first year. Throughout the collaboration, they maintain regular strategy sessions to review progress, share real-time data, and address challenges openly.

To ensure fair collaboration, both partners agree on equitable resource allocation, with the manufacturing firm focusing on production efficiency while the logistics provider manages distribution optimization. They also agree to share risks and rewards proportionally, incentivizing both sides to invest equally in the partnership's success. When a disagreement arises over resource allocation, both partners engage in a constructive dialogue to reassess roles and responsibilities, finding a solution that benefits both sides.

Transparent communication is maintained through regular progress meetings and a shared dashboard where both partners can access key performance metrics, project milestones, and updates in real time. This open dialogue, mutual respect, and clear communication not only help achieve project goals but also build a deeper, more sustainable level of trust over time. This example demonstrates how aligned objectives, fair collaboration, and transparent communication are essential for developing and sustaining trust with partners, aligning with the principles of Trust 360.

Trust with Clients

Trust with clients is foundational to long-term success in any business. While clients are essential to an organization's growth, they are not the only stakeholders that matter. Trust 360 emphasizes that they are one part of a larger ecosystem. Building trust with clients requires more than just providing services or meeting project goals; it involves establishing honest communication, delivering consistent quality, and maintaining respectful boundaries. It is not solely about pleasing them at all costs; it is about forming a transparent, reliable, and mutually beneficial relationship.

Reflecting on a past experience with a large healthcare management company that operated a network of hospitals across a region, we learned that establishing trust with clients can be particularly challenging when clarity and alignment are lacking from the start. The engagement's purpose was clear: to improve operational efficiency and increase patient satisfaction across the hospital network. However, from the outset, we faced a significant barrier: conflicting messages from different client representatives. Each person seemed to have a different version of the problems, with agendas that often appeared disconnected or even contradictory.

This lack of alignment made it difficult for us to navigate the project's scope and deliver solutions that would meet the client's expectations. We struggled with unclear priorities and competing interests, which led to miscommunication and confusion. We knew what quality of service meant to us, but it became apparent that the client had no unified definition of success. Given the fragmented goals and mixed signals, we could not establish a cohesive strategy. In the end, it became evident that the client's leadership was more focused on internal politics than on improving patient outcomes, which ultimately undermined the project's success. It was a tough environment, and despite our efforts, we had to end the engagement prematurely. This experience was a crucial lesson that underscored the importance of clear communication, setting realistic expectations, and establishing mutual understanding in client relationships.

From this challenging project, we learned that client trust is built on three core components: honest communication, quality service, and respectful boundaries.

Honest communication is the foundation of trust in any client relationship. It begins from the very first interaction and must be maintained throughout the engagement. Being upfront about capabilities, timelines, and potential challenges is critical to building realistic expectations from the outset. This level of transparency helps prevent misunderstandings and fosters a stronger working relationship based on mutual respect and shared understanding.

In our experience with the healthcare management company, we failed to establish honest communication early on. The lack of a unified vision from the client's side led to conflicting expectations, which created confusion about what was achievable within the given timeline. In hindsight, it would have been beneficial to conduct a thorough alignment meeting at the start, where all stakeholders could define their goals and agree on what success would look like. By setting realistic expectations about what could be accomplished given the resources, timeline, and organizational dynamics, we might have avoided some of the frustration and confusion that arose later in the project.

Going forward, we made it a standard practice to have clear, upfront discussions about project scope, timelines, and potential limitations. For example, in a subsequent project with another hospital network, we held a kickoff meeting where we discussed possible constraints, such as limited staff availability and tight timelines, which allowed us to align expectations and prioritize efforts more effectively. This transparency built trust early in the relationship, setting the stage for more successful outcomes.

Delivering consistent, high-quality service is another key component of building trust with clients. Quality service goes beyond simply meeting the contractual requirements; it involves exceeding expectations whenever possible and being responsive to client needs as they evolve. However, quality can only be delivered effectively when both parties have a shared understanding of what it means.

In our engagement with the healthcare management company, the disconnect in defining "quality of service" was a major obstacle. While we had a clear understanding of what quality meant to us—timely delivery, thorough analysis, and actionable recommendations—the client's fragmented internal structure meant that there was no consistent standard across their team. Different stakeholders had varied interpretations of what quality should look like, which made it nearly impossible to satisfy everyone's expectations simultaneously.

The result was a misalignment that affected the overall impact of our work. Despite our efforts to maintain high standards, the lack of clear metrics for success on the client's end made it difficult to measure the effectiveness of our interventions. We later learned that establishing a mutually agreed-upon definition of quality is critical to success. In future projects, we introduced a formal process where, early in the engagement, we worked with the client to define specific quality benchmarks, metrics, and outcomes. This ensured that both parties were aligned on what success would look like and how it would be measured. In a similar project with another client in the healthcare sector, we developed a set of clear, measurable indicators of quality, such as reduced patient wait times and improved patient feedback scores. This clarity allowed us to consistently deliver high-quality results that matched the client's expectations, reinforcing trust throughout the engagement.

Maintaining respectful boundaries is essential for sustaining a healthy client relationship and involves managing workloads to ensure that commitments can be met without overextending resources or compromising quality. It also means setting clear limits on what can be achieved within a given timeframe, which helps prevent burnout on both sides and protects the quality of service.

During our engagement with the healthcare management company, we struggled to establish respectful boundaries due to the conflicting demands from various stakeholders. The fragmented nature of the client's organization meant that different departments often had competing priorities, which led to unrealistic demands on our team's time and resources. This misalignment not only affected the quality of service but also caused significant strain on our team. By trying to meet everyone's expectations, we ended up stretching our resources too thin, which compromised the overall effectiveness of our efforts.

In subsequent projects, we learned to set clearer boundaries from the outset. We implemented a phased approach in future engagements, dividing specific deliverables into stages with clear timelines and resource requirements for each phase. This approach helped manage expectations and ensured that both sides were aware of what could realistically be accomplished within the given time and resources. For instance, in a project with a large health insurance provider, we established a clear project roadmap with milestones, timelines, and checkpoints. This allowed us to manage workloads effectively, avoid overextension, and deliver consistent quality without compromising our team's capacity.

A more recent engagement with a hospital network in another region demonstrated the importance of clear communication, consistent quality, and maintaining boundaries. At the start of the project, we conducted a comprehensive kickoff meeting with all key stakeholders, ensuring that everyone had a clear understanding of the project's goals, timelines, and limitations. We defined quality metrics together, agreeing on measurable outcomes like reduced patient wait times and improved patient feedback scores. This alignment helped build trust early on, as both sides shared a common vision of success.

We also implemented a phased approach to the project, with clear milestones and checkpoints along the way. This not only helped manage workloads and prevent overextension but also allowed us to make adjustments based on ongoing feedback, ensuring that we consistently delivered high-quality service that met the client's expectations. The project was a success, with improvements in patient satisfaction scores and more efficient hospital operations. This engagement reinforced the importance of honest communication, defined quality metrics, and clear boundaries, key lessons from our previous challenges that helped us build stronger, more trusting relationships with clients.

By integrating these principles into every client relationship, we not only improve project outcomes but also strengthen the foundation of Trust 360. Establishing trust with clients is not about meeting every demand; it's about creating a relationship based on transparency, mutual respect, and a shared commitment to quality.

Trust with the Community

Building trust with the community is one of the more complex aspects of Trust 360, particularly for a virtual company like ours. Unlike traditional businesses with a single geographic location, our organization operates with a decentralized structure, spread across 17 states and several international locations. As we celebrate our 21st anniversary, it's crucial to consider how we can continue to strengthen trust with diverse communities, despite the challenges of a virtual setup.

Operating virtually has become a new norm across industries, accelerated by the impact of COVID-19. Organizations everywhere—big and small, public and private—have shifted to remote models, recognizing the advantages of flexibility, cost-efficiency, and access to a wider talent pool. What was once a relatively unique approach is now common practice. Our model, though implemented by a relatively small company, is now being adopted by large corporations and governmental organizations alike. This trend underscores the importance of rethinking how community engagement, ethical practices, and transparency are maintained in a virtual context.

The challenge of defining "community" in a virtual organization like ours is unique. With employees working remotely from a wide range of locations and serving clients across different sectors, the concept of community becomes multifaceted. It's not about having one central community; it's about having hundreds of them, each representing different touchpoints through employees, clients, and industry associations.

However, community can be redefined in a broader sense. For us, every client is part of our community, and every association related to the client environment is an extension of that community. For example, when working with a state government agency on disaster recovery efforts, the agency becomes part of our community, as do the citizens it serves. Similarly, when partnering with commercial clients on process improvement, their stakeholders and networks are considered part of our community. This approach emphasizes that every engagement represents an opportunity to build stronger relationships, trust, and positive outcomes, regardless of our physical presence.

Developing trust with the community involves three key elements: community engagement, ethical practices, and transparency.

Community engagement in a virtual organization starts with recognizing that each client and their associated networks are integral parts of the community. Engagement isn't limited to traditional methods, such as sponsoring local events or participating in volunteer days. Instead, it involves meaningful, active participation in the sectors we serve, contributing expertise, resources, and support to enhance broader community outcomes.

For instance, when working on disaster recovery projects for government agencies, we engage not only with the agency but also with local emergency management teams, non-profits, and community leaders. In these scenarios, our role goes beyond fulfilling the contract; we actively contribute to rebuilding efforts by offering expertise in project management, continuous improvement, and strategic planning. By doing so, we establish trust as a reliable community partner committed to more than just business results. We aim to be a contributor to the overall recovery and resilience of the community, regardless of our physical presence.

Additionally, we strengthen community engagement by supporting initiatives that align with our expertise. For example, participating in workshops or panels on process improvement for local government employees or offering strategic planning assistance to non-profits are ways we can contribute to the communities we touch. These engagements not only demonstrate our commitment to community well-being but also help build lasting relationships rooted in trust and shared goals, irrespective of whether interactions happen in person or online.

Adhering to *ethical practices* is central to establishing trust with any community. For a virtual organization like ours, ethical practices mean more than following regulations and compliance standards—they involve a commitment to integrity, fairness, and transparency in every interaction, whether with clients, partners, or broader communities.

Operating across diverse sectors, such as disaster recovery, healthcare management, and economic development, often involves working with vulnerable populations and critical infrastructure. This requires an elevated sense of responsibility and ethical behavior. For example, during disaster recovery efforts, we must ensure that strategies prioritize the needs of affected communities, respect local regulations, and adhere to ethical procurement and deployment of resources. By doing so, we not only fulfill contractual obligations but also demonstrate a commitment to ethical practices that build trust with local agencies, citizens, and other stakeholders.

Ethical behavior also extends to how we interact with industry associations and networks. As part of broader community engagement, we ensure that involvement in these associations promotes integrity and aligns with our core values. Whether participating in policy discussions, advocating for fair practices, or supporting initiatives that drive positive change, maintaining ethical standards in these interactions reinforces our reputation as a trustworthy and principled community partner.

Transparency is vital for building trust with any community, but it becomes even more critical for a virtual company, where the absence of physical presence can sometimes make trust harder to establish. Transparency must be woven into every aspect of our work, from client interactions to broader community engagements.

One way transparency manifests is through open communication with clients about project goals, progress, and challenges. For example, when implementing process improvement initiatives in a network of hospitals, we ensure that all stakeholders—whether hospital administrators, medical staff, or patient advocates—have access to clear information about the project's status, anticipated outcomes, and any potential roadblocks. By keeping communication channels open and consistent, we reinforce trust and demonstrate accountability, which is essential when serving communities that depend on the outcomes of our work.

Transparency is also about being honest and clear about the organization's impact in the sectors it serves. As we interact with various communities— be it through disaster recovery, economic development, or healthcare improvements—it's important to ensure that contributions are well-documented and openly shared. For instance, in a project supporting economic recovery in a distressed region, we could publish progress reports or case studies that highlight not only successes but also lessons learned. By sharing insights and outcomes openly, we position ourselves as a transparent partner that values collaboration and continuous improvement.

One of the best examples of community engagement is our work in disaster recovery across different states. In a recent engagement with a state emergency management agency, we recognized the importance of building trust not just with the client but also with the broader community it served. We began by engaging with local officials, non-profits, and community leaders to understand their needs and expectations. This proactive involvement enabled us to tailor solutions that better served affected populations, demonstrating our investment in the community's well-being, not just in fulfilling contractual obligations.

Throughout the project, we adhered to strict ethical standards, ensuring that resources were allocated fairly and transparently. We also maintained consistent communication with all stakeholders, sharing updates on progress, challenges, and milestones achieved. By doing so, we built trust with the state agency, local community leaders, and the citizens directly impacted by our work.

This approach reinforced the broader principles of Trust 360: engaging meaningfully with the community, maintaining ethical practices, and ensuring transparency at every step. As we continue to enhance our virtual work environment and build trust across various communities, the lessons learned from this and similar projects will guide efforts to become a more integrated and reliable community partner. By recognizing that every client, sector, and stakeholder network forms part of our community, we can continue to foster trust and create positive, lasting change wherever we operate, no matter how remote our presence may be.

Implementing Trust 360

The relationships we cultivate with our team members, clients, partners, and communities are the cornerstones of our success. Trust 360 is more than a set of principles; it's a comprehensive strategy guiding how we interact, make decisions, and develop relationships at every level. As we move forward, leadership is committed to fostering a culture of trust and servant leadership within our organization. By strengthening trust at all levels, we can create a more positive and productive work environment that not only drives performance but also sustains long-term growth.

Implementing Trust 360 is an ongoing process, requiring deliberate actions and a deep organizational commitment. It's not a one-time initiative but a continuous process that evolves as relationships grow. After learning from past challenges, we adopted specific Trust 360 policies to rebuild and enhance relationships with all stakeholders. These policies include regular employee feedback sessions, restructured workloads to prevent burnout, re-engagement with partners through collaborative projects, and active participation in the communities we serve. Each of these efforts represents a step toward making Trust 360 a core part of our organizational DNA.

To make Trust 360 effective, we focus on three core strategies: balanced decision-making, culture building, and continuous improvement.

Balanced decision-making is essential to Trust 360, ensuring that the needs and perspectives of employees, clients, partners, and communities are considered in every decision. It aims to promote fairness and equity, creating an environment where all stakeholders feel valued. This approach not only fosters trust but also helps prevent imbalances that can lead to frustration or disengagement.

A critical component of balanced decision-making is the 80-20 strategy, part of the 10X Strategy discussed earlier in this book. This strategy focuses on expanding the 20% of tasks that employees excel at, enjoy, and have a significant impact on, while reducing the remaining 80% of tasks that may contribute to stress or disengagement. Incorporating "hidden gems"—tasks that bring unexpected value and align with employees' strengths—further enhances satisfaction and prevents burnout.

For example, when evaluating employee workloads, we now prioritize tasks that align with their skills and passions. If a team member excels at client communication and enjoys problem-solving, we adjust their responsibilities to focus more on these strengths, which drives both job satisfaction and better outcomes. This approach not only reduces burnout but also increases engagement, productivity, and overall performance. By ensuring that decision-making reflects a thoughtful consideration of what benefits all stakeholders, we create a more balanced, supportive, and effective work environment.

Culture building is a foundational element of implementing Trust 360. Leadership plays a vital role in modeling trust-building behaviors, setting the tone for an organization-wide commitment to openness, transparency, and mutual respect. Trust is not just a stated value; it must be actively demonstrated in daily interactions and practices.

To foster this culture, we introduced several initiatives that emphasize open communication, empowerment, and recognition. Regular feedback sessions have become central to our operations, providing employees with opportunities to voice concerns, share ideas, and suggest improvements without fear of retribution. During feedback meetings, employees can provide candid input on workload distribution, project challenges, and overall job satisfaction. Leaders use this feedback to inform decisions about resource allocation, training needs, and professional development, reinforcing a culture of openness and trust.

Recognition has also played a crucial role in strengthening this culture. We make it a point to publicly acknowledge and celebrate behaviors that build trust, such as transparency, collaboration, and innovative problem-solving. By shining a spotlight on these actions, we reinforce the organization's commitment to trust-building and encourage others to model similar behaviors.

Leadership also promotes a sense of belonging and inclusion by participating in team-building activities, mentoring programs, and cross-departmental collaboration. These efforts help create an environment where employees feel connected, supported, and valued, reinforcing trust at every level of the organization.

Continuous improvement is a central pillar of Trust 360, ensuring that trust remains strong and resilient as relationships evolve. It involves creating clear feedback channels for employees, clients, partners, and community members, allowing for ongoing input and dialogue. This openness to feedback not only supports stronger relationships but also drives ongoing adaptation and growth.

In response to past challenges, we focused on creating consistent feedback loops inside the organization. Rather than relying on formal surveys, we built habits of ongoing dialogue, whether through one-on-one check-ins, team retrospectives, or leadership roundtables. These conversations helped surface concerns early, clarify expectations, and uncover opportunities for improvement in real time. By responding quickly and transparently, we showed our team that their input was valued and acted upon, strengthening trust and collaboration.

Continuous improvement also became part of how we worked together day-to-day. From refining internal processes to streamlining project delivery, we encouraged team members to identify friction points and propose solutions. Many of these ideas emerged through our monthly

Idea Pitch program, where employees could present suggestions directly to leadership for immediate consideration. This practice not only improved efficiency but also deepened ownership, demonstrating that innovation and trust grow strongest when everyone has a seat at the table.

Regular assessments are vital for maintaining trust. Ongoing performance reviews now include not only project outcomes but also evaluations of how well trust was maintained throughout the engagement. These reviews identify best practices, areas for growth, and opportunities to strengthen relationships. By consistently evaluating our efforts and making necessary adjustments, we ensure that trust remains a central focus of our operations and relationships.

Looking Forward

Implementing Trust 360 is not just about addressing past challenges; it's about laying a strong foundation for the future. By embracing balanced decision-making, culture-building, and continuous improvement, we aim to create relationships that are transparent, resilient, and mutually beneficial. Trust 360 is more than just a strategy; it's a commitment to building an organization where trust guides every interaction, decision, and relationship. As we continue to enhance trust at all levels, we foster a more positive and productive work environment that supports sustainable growth and long-term success.

The benefits of Trust 360 are extensive and transformative, impacting every aspect of the organization. By focusing on cultivating trust in all directions, we've seen measurable improvements in areas that directly contribute to long-term success. Implementing Trust 360 has led to a more cohesive and engaged workforce, stronger partnerships, and a well-respected reputation among clients and the communities we serve. These benefits not only drive performance but also create a resilient foundation that supports sustainable growth. The positive changes we experienced were clear across multiple dimensions:

Enhanced Reputation: As trust became central to our operations, it improved our standing with both clients and partners. By consistently demonstrating integrity, transparency, and fairness, we established a reputation as a reliable and ethical organization. This enhanced reputation helped us attract new clients, solidify existing relationships, and open doors to new opportunities. Clients now see us not just as service providers but as trusted partners committed to mutual success.

Increased Employee Satisfaction: Trust 360 had a profound impact on employee engagement and satisfaction. As we implemented policies that prioritized open communication, empowerment, and work-life balance, employees felt more valued and supported. The 80-20 strategy, for example, allowed employees to focus more on the tasks they were good at, enjoyed, and that made an impact. This not only reduced burnout but also increased job satisfaction and motivation. Employees felt a greater sense of ownership and purpose, resulting in higher productivity and lower turnover rates.

Stronger Partnerships: The collaborative nature of Trust 360 enhanced our relationships with partners. By aligning goals, ensuring fair collaboration, and maintaining transparent communication, we fostered deeper, more effective partnerships. Partners became increasingly invested in joint success, leading to more innovative solutions and better outcomes for clients. This stronger partnership dynamic also allowed us to pursue more ambitious projects and expand our service offerings with greater confidence.

Solid Community Support: Our redefined approach to community engagement—treating every client, sector, and stakeholder as part of our broader community—created new networks and stronger connections. Active participation in community initiatives, combined with ethical practices and transparent communication, helped us establish trust and credibility. This solid community support not only reinforced our impact but also provided valuable insights and feedback, helping us refine our strategies and adapt to the needs of diverse communities.

As we continue to implement Trust 360, these benefits reinforce the organization's resilience and adaptability, creating an environment where success is shared and sustained. Trust 360 is not just about achieving short-term gains; it's about building lasting relationships that empower everyone involved, including employees, clients, partners, and communities, to thrive.

Our experience has shown us that prioritizing one stakeholder at the expense of others is a flawed strategy. By focusing too narrowly on the needs of one group, whether it's clients, employees, or partners, we risk neglecting the larger ecosystem that supports long-term success. Trust cannot be selectively applied; it must be cultivated in all directions. Trust 360 represents a commitment to building and maintaining trust across every relationship, from team members to clients, partners, and the broader community. By embracing this holistic approach, we create a balanced, harmonious environment where everyone thrives. This balance not only prevents burnout and misalignment but also fosters sustainable success that benefits the entire organization.

Trust 360 is more than a theoretical framework; it is a practice we have embedded into the fabric of our company. It enables us to anticipate challenges, build resilient relationships, and ensure that every decision is made with fairness and transparency. The result is an organizational culture where trust drives performance, collaboration, and innovation, and where every stakeholder feels valued and respected.

The pivot from a narrow, client-focused approach to the holistic Trust 360 model was a groundbreaking shift. It allowed us to strengthen every aspect of our organization, ensuring that we operate from a resilient foundation built on trust and mutual respect. Trust is not built overnight; it requires consistent actions that demonstrate integrity, transparency, and fairness in every interaction. We've seen firsthand how, by committing to Trust 360, we can navigate the complexities of the business world more effectively, ensuring that success is shared, sustained, and scalable.

This experience has taught us that trust is not a finite resource to be directed at one stakeholder group, but a foundational element that connects all parts of the organization. By nurturing trust with employees, partners, clients, and the community, we create an environment that fosters collaboration, innovation, and long-term growth. Trust 360 allows us to respond to challenges with agility and confidence, knowing that the relationships we've built are strong and capable of withstanding the inevitable pressures of business.

Key Takeaways

- Prioritizing one stakeholder at the expense of others creates imbalances that can lead to organizational decline. Trust must be cultivated equally across all relationships, with employees, partners, clients, and the community.
- Implementing Trust 360 requires deliberate strategies, including balanced decision-making, culture building, and continuous improvement. These strategies result in enhanced organizational reputation, greater employee satisfaction, stronger partnerships, and increased community support.

Action Steps

- **Assess current trust levels:** Begin by evaluating the state of trust with each stakeholder group: employees, clients, partners, and the community.

- **Engage in open dialogue:** Initiate conversations that foster honest feedback and open communication, allowing for transparency and clarity.
- **Develop trust-building plans:** Create deliberate strategies that align with Trust 360 principles, ensuring that trust is nurtured across all relationships.
- **Monitor and adjust:** Regularly evaluate trust levels and outcomes, making adjustments as necessary to reinforce and strengthen relationships over time.

By adopting Trust 360, organizations can create a lasting legacy of integrity, fairness, and success. The positive impact of this approach will resonate through every interaction, driving sustainable growth and empowering the organization to thrive in a complex and dynamic world.

Trust 360 gave us more than a framework; it gave us a new lens on every relationship. Still, we soon realized that building trust wasn't enough. To sustain it, we needed a way to focus our energy and ensure people were spending their time where it mattered most. That's when the 80/20 principle became a key tool for our leadership.

Leveraging the 80/20 Rule

Trust 360 provided a framework for building stronger relationships, but it also revealed a deeper challenge: how to help people focus their energy on areas that create the most value once trust is established? That question first came into sharp focus during one of our earliest large training engagements.

A Room Divided

In the early days of our company, a significant portion of our work was centered around corporate training—engaging with large organizations to help them improve operational performance, leadership behaviors, and culture. One particular training session from that era remains etched in my memory, not because everything went smoothly, but because it taught us more about human nature and organizational dysfunction than perhaps any other engagement before or since.

We were working with a large, complex organization comprising several divisions, each with its own priorities, internal pressures, and legacy issues. For this engagement, we had been contracted to deliver a two-week intensive training, split into two one-week sessions spaced a month apart, focused on continuous process improvement.

From the outset, the dynamics in the room felt off. We had four large round tables set up, each occupied by participants from a different division. While this setup was intentionally designed to support our group exercises and encourage diverse collaboration, what we observed instead was isolation. Each group kept to itself, physically, emotionally, and mentally. There was a palpable tension in the air. It wasn't long before minor disagreements turned into sharp exchanges between tables. Comments became passive-aggressive. Snide remarks were made about how certain divisions made other people's jobs harder, or how work was constantly being thrown "over the fence" with no accountability. You could feel the collective mood souring by the hour.

As trainers, we were used to encountering some resistance. After all, change is uncomfortable. But this was different. As I listened more closely, I began to notice a troubling undercurrent; not just interdepartmental friction, but an overwhelming sense of *disillusionment* with the work itself. People were openly venting that they spent their days doing tasks they didn't enjoy, didn't feel they were good at, or didn't believe had any real impact. They were burned out, cynical, and often resigned to the idea that "this is just how things are." By the afternoon of that first day, the situation escalated to the point where curse words started flying. We had completely lost the room.

My co-trainer and I quickly huddled. We knew we couldn't continue as planned, not in that environment. With the support of the facility organizer, we secured an additional training room and divided the class in half. It wasn't ideal, but it gave us the space we needed to de-escalate. With the smaller groups, we stepped back from the curriculum entirely and simply opened the floor for conversation. We invited participants to share how they were really feeling—not about the training, but about their work. What emerged in those conversations was deeply revealing. People spoke about how little joy or fulfillment they found in their roles.

They were frustrated not just with broken processes or other departments, but with the reality that most of their day-to-day work felt like a poor fit for their strengths.

What struck me most was how many of them couldn't clearly articulate what they actually enjoyed doing, or what they were really good at. We weren't even talking solutions at this point. We were just listening. It became less of a training and more of a therapeutic space. There were moments of silence. Moments of tears. But also, moments of real honesty. And it started to click for me: what we were seeing was not a failure of collaboration, but a failure of alignment. People were being asked to spend the majority of their time in what we now refer to as their 80% zone—doing work they didn't enjoy, weren't especially skilled at, and didn't believe mattered. No wonder the mood was toxic. No wonder the smallest request from another division felt like a personal attack.

At the end of that week, we didn't have a perfect resolution. But we had a calmer room, and a shared understanding that something deeper needed to shift. We sent participants back to their work with a challenge: to reflect on what it would look like if more of their time—ideally, most of it—was spent on tasks they loved, were capable of doing well, and saw as making a real impact. That framing changed everything. When we returned a month later for the second week of the training, the atmosphere was noticeably different. People came in more open, more thoughtful, more grounded. They had taken the assignment seriously. They had journaled, discussed with peers, and even tested new approaches at work.

This time, we went deeper. Using an organizational chart template, we asked each person to mark their current roles and tasks in one of three colors: **green** for the work they enjoyed, excelled at, and found meaningful; **yellow** for work they were neutral about; and **red** for tasks that felt misaligned or draining. The first week, most charts were bleeding red. Now, we began to see shifts—more green, more yellow, and people actively discussing how to convert red tasks by trading responsibilities, rethinking processes, or simply giving themselves permission to question longstanding assumptions.

The most powerful insight came not from top-down restructuring, but from lateral conversations. Participants realized that one person's red task was another's green. Tasks that had felt like burdens for years were being handed off to someone who actually loved doing them. This was the real magic. We weren't just redesigning processes; we were rediscovering people's strengths and honoring them. By the end of the second week, there was laughter in the room. There was cooperation. There was hope. The lines between divisions had started to blur—not because we mandated unity, but because people had begun to operate from a place of trust, purpose, and choice.

That training session left a lasting impression on me. It was one of the earliest and clearest signals of what would later become our application of the 80/20 rule. Though we didn't call it that at the time, what we witnessed was the profound shift that occurs when people spend more time doing what they're built to do. It wasn't just about productivity; it was about healing, about rehumanizing the workplace, about designing jobs around the person rather than the other way around. And once you've seen what's possible, you can't unsee it. That experience fundamentally changed how we approach leadership, and it laid the groundwork for the 10X strategy we practice today.

What we witnessed in that training room was not unique to that organization. It was a mirror for us as well. Back at our own company, we began asking the same questions: *Are our people spending most of their time in their green zone, or stuck in the red?* That reflection prompted us to reassess our roles, responsibilities, and even our own leadership habits. The 80/20 principle became more than a training exercise. It became a framework for how we structured work, empowered team members, and measured success.

The 80/20 Rule, Reframed

Most people are familiar with the 80/20 rule, also known as the *Pareto Principle:* the idea that approximately 80% of outcomes stem from 20% of efforts. In the business world, this concept is often used to highlight that a small number of clients drive most of the revenue, or that a few tasks produce the majority of results. But in our leadership practice, we've redefined the 80/20 rule not as a mathematical observation, but as a human one.

We use the 80/20 rule to examine how people spend their time and energy, both at work and in life, and how aligned those activities are with three essential criteria:

1. Do you enjoy doing it?
2. Are you capable and well-trained to do it well?
3. Do you believe it makes a meaningful impact?

Only when all three of these are true does a task belong in your 20% zone. Everything else—what drains you, distracts you, or simply doesn't align—falls into the 80%. Most people, without even realizing it, spend the majority of their day stuck in that 80% zone. And that's where disengagement, burnout, and miscommunication take root.

We've found that identifying this divide is not enough. You have to name it, map it, and then redesign around it. That's why we've incorporated structured 80/20 assessments into our leadership workshops. One of the most impactful applications of this came nearly two years ago, when I facilitated a series of internal strategy sessions with our management team.

Almost 18 years after that first memorable training session described earlier in this chapter, I found myself guiding our own leaders through the same lens of the 80/20 framework, only this time with deeper intent. Each manager was challenged to evaluate not only their professional responsibilities but also their personal lives through this lens. What are the tasks you truly enjoy doing? Where do you feel most capable and confident? And where do you sense your contribution creates meaningful impact?

They were asked to make two lists: one for work and one for life outside of work. I made it clear that they wouldn't have to share their personal list—this was meant for their own reflection. But something unexpected and powerful happened. As one manager chose to speak up and share a personal insight, others followed. The room transformed. People began sharing vulnerably, not just about operational tasks or project work, but about their relationships, families, and sense of purpose. One team member, holding back tears, shared how they longed to spend more quality time with a child. That comment cracked the room open. What was meant to be a tactical strategy session turned into something far more human: a moment of shared vulnerability that deepened trust across the leadership team.

I joined in, too. I talked about my own 80/20, not just in my role as a president, but as a father, a son, a person still on my own growth journey. What emerged wasn't just an alignment of tasks; it was an alignment of values. For many, it became a turning point. Several people made quiet but bold decisions in the weeks that followed—to delegate differently, to reprioritize their time, to say no to things they had previously accepted as inevitable. One even reorganized their personal calendar to make space for more green-zone activities with family. Another restructured team roles to empower a direct report who had been waiting for the opportunity to take on more.

What that session taught me—and reaffirmed for all of us—is that the 80/20 rule is about far more than productivity. It is a gateway to clarity, fulfillment, and sustainable performance. When people begin to see that meaningful work doesn't have to be rare or occasional, that it can, with intention, become the norm, they start showing up differently. They bring more energy. They become more generous. They lead more effectively.

To move from awareness to action, we incorporate several tools and techniques:

- **The 80/20 Activity Canvas** to map tasks and responsibilities.
- **The Red-Yellow-Green Chart** to visualize energy alignment across roles.
- **Hidden Gems Brainstorming** to identify tasks that aren't currently being done but should be, often sitting dormant just outside the daily grind.
- **The 4 Cs Framework**—Commitment, Courage, Capability, and Confidence—to address the psychological barriers that keep us in our 80%.

Each of these tools serves one purpose: to re-center people on what they are *meant* to be doing. We've seen firsthand that when an organization makes this shift—not just at the individual level, but at scale—it becomes something more than a workplace. It becomes a place of growth, trust, and shared purpose. Now, let's break down these tools in more detail.

The 80/20 Activity Canvas:
Mapping Tasks and Responsibilities

The 80/20 Activity Canvas is the foundational tool we use to surface how aligned or misaligned someone's daily activities are with their strengths and values. Most people operate on autopilot, moving from task to task without pausing to assess whether what they're doing is something they actually enjoy, are skilled at, or feel makes a meaningful difference. This canvas invites them to step back and take inventory. The process begins by listing out all their recurring activities, both professional and personal, and then evaluating each one against three simple but powerful criteria: *Do I enjoy doing this? Am I capable and well-prepared to do it well? Does it contribute to something meaningful or impactful?*

Only when all three conditions are met does a task belong in the 20% column. Anything that falls short in one or more areas goes into the 80% bucket. What emerges from this exercise is often surprising. Even seasoned leaders discover that a large percentage of their time is consumed by work that doesn't energize them, doesn't leverage their strengths, and doesn't connect to what they truly care about. It's not just a matter of inefficiency; it's a drain on morale and performance.

But the goal of this canvas isn't just awareness. It's to spark redesign. Once the tasks are mapped, leaders can begin reimagining how to redistribute work across the team. Tasks in someone's 80% zone may fall squarely in someone else's 20%. This opens up powerful conversations about delegation, empowerment, and alignment. It also prompts critical reflection about legacy responsibilities: *Are we doing things just because we've always done them? Are we hoarding tasks that others would thrive doing?* The canvas helps shift that mindset and create a culture where people are deployed according to their strengths, not just their job titles.

The Red-Yellow-Green Chart:
Visualizing Energy Alignment

If the canvas helps individuals articulate what fits and what doesn't, the Red-Yellow-Green Chart helps them *see* it. It changes the qualitative insights from the canvas into a simple, color-coded diagnostic tool that provides instant clarity. Each task or responsibility is categorized into one of three colors: Green represents the work someone enjoys, excels at, and believes to be impactful. Yellow stands for neutral work, tasks they tolerate or feel indifferent toward. Red indicates the work that drains them, lies outside their capability zone, or feels disconnected from any meaningful outcome.

What makes this chart so powerful is how it turns abstract feelings into something visual, concrete, and shareable. When a team creates these charts together, a deeper understanding begins to emerge, both about individuals and about the system they're operating in. Managers often discover that large portions of their job have turned red over time, not because the work changed, but because *they* have evolved. Some leaders notice that their team members are shouldering too much red without ever raising their hands. Others begin to recognize areas of misalignment across departments or functions that they had previously chalked up to "personality issues" or "communication gaps."

This tool also normalizes the reality that roles need to evolve. No one should be expected to operate indefinitely in red. And yellow shouldn't be ignored; it's a sign that something could either move toward green with the right support, or drift toward red without it. The goal isn't to eliminate all red or yellow, but to ensure that people spend the majority of their time in green, and that the organization is structured to make that possible. Used regularly, the Red-Yellow-Green Chart becomes more than a tool; it becomes a language for alignment, performance, and renewal.

Hidden Gems Brainstorming: Discovering Untapped Potential

Once people begin to reclaim time from their 80%, a natural question arises: *What would I do with the freed-up space?* This is where Hidden Gems Brainstorming comes into play. It's an exercise designed to surface the high-impact, high-energy work that people aren't currently doing but would love to do if given the opportunity. These "gems" are typically buried beneath layers of responsibility, routine, and reactive demands. They may not appear on any official job description, but they represent the kind of work that can embody both personal fulfillment and organizational value.

We ask participants to take 15-20 minutes to reflect on ideas that have been sitting in the back of their minds, things they're passionate about but haven't had the time, authority, or headspace to pursue. The results are often remarkable. People list projects, process improvements, new service ideas, innovations, and contributions that have the potential to create 10X the impact. Some want to mentor others. Some want to redesign outdated systems. Others want to explore new technologies, connect more directly with clients, or build entirely new initiatives that align with the company's mission.

The key insight here is that people are not disengaged because they don't care; they're disengaged because their best ideas have no outlet. By creating a structured space for Hidden Gems, leaders send a message: *We see you. We trust you. We want your whole self at work.* The power of this tool lies in its future orientation. While the canvas and chart help diagnose the present, hidden gems shape the future. They open up space for innovation, succession planning, personal growth, and, most importantly, renewed energy.

The 4 Cs Framework:
Overcoming the Barriers to Change

Even when people gain insight about their 20%, visualize their alignment, and name their hidden gems, many still hesitate to make changes. Why? Because change, especially the kind that involves identity, control, and vulnerability, requires more than knowledge. It requires confronting a set of deeply human barriers that we've come to call the 4 Cs: Commitment, Courage, Capability, and Confidence.

Commitment is the starting point. It's easy to say you want to focus on your 20%; it's much harder to commit to it when the emails keep coming, the meetings keep stacking, and the demands of the day threaten to derail your focus. True commitment requires setting boundaries, saying no to work that falls outside your zone, and resisting the pull of urgent-but-unimportant tasks. It's a discipline that must be practiced daily and modeled visibly by leadership.

Courage is what allows people to take the first step into something unfamiliar. Letting go of long-held responsibilities, raising your hand for something new, or admitting that you've outgrown part of your role requires vulnerability. Many leaders stay stuck in their 80% not because they want to but because they're afraid of appearing weak, dispensable, or exposed. Creating a psychologically safe environment where courage is celebrated, not punished, is a key leadership responsibility.

Capability represents the skills gap that sometimes exists between where someone is and where they want to be. A person may have the desire to shift into their 20%, but lack training, mentorship, or resources to grow into it. Leaders must recognize this and build capability bridges through learning opportunities, peer coaching, or realigned stretch assignments. No one should be penalized for wanting to step into their potential.

Confidence is the final gate. It's the internal belief that *I belong in this work*. Even with support and resources, people won't shift into their 20% unless they believe they can deliver and that their contribution is valued. Confidence is built incrementally through successful small wins, honest feedback, and the encouragement of peers and leaders. It is the emotional fuel that sustains momentum.

When an organization embraces the 4 Cs as part of its culture, transformation becomes not only possible but inevitable. People move with clarity and energy. Teams reorient around shared strengths. And leadership becomes a vehicle for unlocking potential, not managing constraints.

Bringing It All Together:
Tools in Service of Trust and Transformation

Taken individually, the 80/20 Activity Canvas, the Red-Yellow-Green Chart, Hidden Gems Brainstorming, and the 4 Cs Framework are powerful tools for personal insight and team alignment. But when they are used together within the context of a leadership model grounded in trust and service, they become something far greater. They become a system for transformation.

These tools also reflect the heart of servant leadership: the belief that a leader's role is not to command from above but to unlock potential from within. When a leader creates space for someone to offload a draining task, or champions their hidden gem, or supports them through the 4 Cs, that is an act of service. It's also an act of strategy, because when people are aligned with what they love, are skilled at, and believe matters, performance becomes exponential. Engagement becomes intrinsic. Retention becomes natural.

This is not about chasing perfection or achieving some utopian workplace where every moment is green. It's about making progress visible, trust actionable, and work personal again. These frameworks allow us to do just that—not as a one-time exercise, but as an ongoing practice that adapts with each person, each team, and each season of growth.

Looking back, I can see that what started as a training method became a way of leading. What began as a conversation about efficiency became a path toward fulfillment. And what once felt like a theory became, over time, one of the most human and impactful strategies we've ever embraced. The 80/20 principle gave us a lens. These tools gave us the structure. But trust, earned and shared, was always the bridge.

The Power of Reclaiming the 20%

The 80/20 rule began as an observation about economics, but in the context of leadership, it has become a profound metaphor for how we allocate not just our time, but our energy, potential, and identity. We now understand that the 20% is not just a slice of our schedule where we're more efficient, it's the zone where we are most alive, most engaged, and most capable of making a lasting impact. When people are operating in their 20%, they aren't just getting more done; they are moving from transaction to transformation. This is where creativity thrives, collaboration becomes effortless, and fulfillment starts to take root. It's not about squeezing more output from the same hours; it's about realigning the work to fit the person, not forcing the person to fit the work.

Throughout this chapter, we've explored practical tools for identifying and expanding that 20% zone, starting with the 80/20 Activity Canvas, which surfaces misalignments that often go unnoticed. We've examined how the Red-Yellow-Green Chart brings visibility to emotional energy in the workplace, offering a visual vocabulary for difficult but necessary conversations. We introduced Hidden Gems Brainstorming as a means of unlocking dormant ideas and ambitions that hold the key to 10X growth. And we unpacked the 4 Cs—Commitment, Courage, Capability, and Confidence—as the internal gatekeepers that determine whether change becomes a reality or remains an aspiration. These tools are simple in structure, but profound in their ability to unlock momentum and human potential.

What we've also seen again and again is that real change doesn't come from process optimization alone. It comes from trust. When a team member sees that their leader cares enough to ask what work brings them alive, something shifts. When a manager openly admits that a portion of their own job has turned red, it sets a tone of honesty and psychological safety. These are not minor gestures; they are cultural signals. They tell people that they are not just valued for what they produce, but for who they are. And that message, when lived consistently, builds a foundation of loyalty, innovation, and sustained performance that no external incentive can match.

Perhaps most moving are the quiet personal revelations that emerge during this work. In nearly every 80/20 session we've facilitated, whether with clients or within our own company, someone inevitably breaks the surface with a reflection that takes the room by surprise. A story about time lost with family. A passion that was shelved for the sake of obligation. A dream still lingering in the background. These moments remind us that the work we do isn't just professional—it's personal. Our jobs are not separate from our lives. The energy we lose in misalignment spills over into our homes, our relationships, and our sense of self-worth. The gift of reclaiming your 20% is not just higher productivity; it's emotional recalibration. It's returning to a version of yourself that feels whole.

As leaders, we have a choice: we can continue to push people harder within outdated structures, or we can redesign those structures to serve human thriving. The 80/20 framework is not a quick fix or a quarterly tactic—it's a long-term philosophy of trust, humility, and intentional design. When we create space for people to do what they are good at, what they enjoy, and what they believe truly matters, we don't just build better organizations, we build better lives. That is the real ROI. And that is the kind of leadership the future demands.

Chapter 5 Summary: Applying the 80/20 Leadership Tools

Framework Overview

TOOL	PURPOSE	OUTCOME
80/20 Activity Canvas	Map daily activities to identify what aligns with passion, skill, and impact	Reveals current task alignment and creates opportunity for redesign
Red-Yellow-Green Chart	Visualize energy and engagement across all tasks	Makes misalignment visible and opens space for realignment
Hidden Gems Brainstorming	Surface untapped high-impact activities	Unlocks innovation and creates pathways for intrinsic motivation
The 4 Cs Framework	Address psychological barriers to working in the 20% zone	Builds commitment, courage, capability, and confidence for lasting change
Core Principle:	**Work that energizes is work that multiplies.** Aligning tasks with what people enjoy, are capable of, and believe matters transforms culture from the inside out.	

Reflection Prompt: For Leaders and Teams

Personal Reflection	• What percentage of your time today is truly spent in your 20% zone? • Which tasks drain your energy or feel misaligned—and why are you still doing them? • What's one hidden gem that's been on your mind that you haven't yet made time for?
Team Reflection	• How well do you know your team's individual 20% zones? • What tasks could be reassigned or traded to create more alignment? • What structures or conversations do you need to initiate to begin mining hidden gems?

The lesson of the 80/20 principle was simple but profound: impact multiplies when people spend more of their time in the work they love, excel at, and find meaningful. By deliberately shifting energy toward the 20% that truly matters, we unlocked not just productivity but also trust, creativity, and fulfillment across the organization.

Once we understood the power of focusing on the 20%, the next question became clear: How do we ensure that each team member is positioned to bring their best strengths to the work that matters most? That is what we explore in the next chapter: aligning roles, responsibilities, and opportunities with the unique strengths of every individual.

CHAPTER 6

Aligning Strengths with Organizational Goals

A key to our evolution was encouraging team members to engage in work that aligned with their strengths and interests. This alignment led to improved performance, job satisfaction, and a sense of belonging, creating an environment where motivation and productivity thrived. It fostered a culture of innovation and commitment, where team members felt valued and impactful.

But alignment wasn't accidental—it was intentional. We began by mapping individual 20% zones, the unique mix of tasks that energized people, drew on their innate talents, and made them feel like their work mattered. These zones were not always tied to job titles or traditional roles. In fact, some of the most powerful breakthroughs occurred when individuals were encouraged to step outside their formal job description and contribute from a place of personal genius.

Once we uncovered these zones of genius, the next step was to overlay them with our organizational goals. This was where the magic happened. Rather than forcing people to mold themselves into rigid roles, we reimagined roles based on what people did best. We shifted the question from *"How can we fill this role?"* to *"How can this person's strengths help us reach our strategic priorities?"* It created a dynamic model of alignment, one where growth was two-sided: individual growth fueling organizational growth, and vice versa.

A Story of Misalignment and Growth

During the early days of my consulting practice, I was hired by a major oil company to help restructure its transportation division. The organization was mired in bureaucracy, and siloed operations were the norm. I was brought in by the Vice President of Strategy and Organizational Development—let's call him John—to conduct a full diagnostic of the division and assess whether the people in leadership positions were aligned with their responsibilities.

Over the course of several weeks, I sat in on leadership meetings, interviewed executives individually, and observed how decisions were made. What John described during our initial conversation turned out to be entirely accurate. The company had recently undergone a series of acquisitions and a large merger. In the rush to stabilize operations, roles had been filled based on convenience or availability rather than strategic alignment. Leaders were operating day to day, often firefighting, and both morale and performance were suffering as a result. The misalignment wasn't malicious; it was just never properly addressed.

However, as the project progressed, I came to realize that John had a secondary agenda. While his stated goal was to improve organizational effectiveness, he also hoped the assessment would justify his own promotion to VP of Operations, a role with significantly more power and compensation. But despite his talents in strategy, John wasn't the right fit for that role. He lacked the operational mindset and frontline credibility needed to succeed there.

When I delivered my final report, a candid and detailed roadmap for realignment, John thanked me, but made no move to implement the recommendations. I didn't hear from him again and assumed the engagement had been shelved. It felt like being quietly fired. Then, a year later, he resurfaced. He told me they had finally acted on the recommendations and made many of the changes I had proposed. He also admitted that he had come to realize he wasn't the right fit for the operations role; a difficult but mature realization that allowed the organization to move forward.

This experience taught me something crucial: alignment between strengths and roles cannot be forced. When it is, everyone pays a price. It also reminded me that true transformation is as much about personal growth as it is about structural change. John's journey and the organization's delay in making the necessary shifts highlight how deeply human these issues are.

Why These Tools Matter

Stories like this underscore why tools like the 80/20 Canvas, the Red-Yellow-Green Chart, Hidden Gems Brainstorming, and the 4Cs Framework aren't just theoretical exercises; they are essential instruments for unlocking real alignment. Had that organization used these tools early on, the misalignment could have been spotted and addressed long before it turned into a costly drain on morale and performance. The Canvas would have revealed the mismatch between duties and capabilities. The Chart would have highlighted where leaders were disengaged or drained by tasks for which they were unsuited. Hidden Gems would have surfaced overlooked talent or reassignments that could have energized the team. And the 4Cs Framework could have helped John and others confront the uncomfortable reality of misfit roles with clarity and humility. These tools empower both individuals and organizations to engage in honest conversations and make bold, informed decisions. They help leaders shift from wishful thinking to thoughtful alignment, a critical leap for any high-performing organization.

The story of John and the oil company is not just about misalignment; it's a lesson in trust. At its core, Trust 360 is about building and sustaining trust in every direction: leaders to team members, team members to leadership, individuals to themselves, and the organization to its mission. When any one of these relationships is misaligned, trust begins to erode.

In this case, John's intentions were mixed. He sought both organizational improvement and personal advancement. That dual motive, left unspoken, created an invisible layer of mistrust. Even though the organization trusted me enough to conduct the assessment, and I trusted them to act on the findings, the process stalled, not because of data, but due to unacknowledged misalignment between aspiration and capability. This is where Trust 360 could have changed the outcome.

If Trust 360 had been embedded in the culture, John might have felt safe enough to articulate his goals openly and engage in a conversation about fit, not just for others, but for himself. He could have reflected honestly on whether the operations role aligned with his natural strengths. Likewise, leadership across the organization could have fostered transparency rather than compliance and modeled what it looks like to put organizational needs over personal ambition without shame or penalty. Trust 360 invites us to hold space for both ambition and honesty, growth and humility.

Analysis and Learning

Trust is the Foundation for Alignment

Real alignment—between people and roles, and between individual strengths and organizational goals—cannot happen in a culture of fear or secrecy. Trust 360 creates the conditions for truth to surface. It allows people to speak candidly about what they're good at, what drains them, and where they truly want to contribute. Without trust, tools like the Canvas and Red-Yellow-Green Chart become checkboxes instead of catalysts.

Unspoken Agendas Break the Loop

When team members pursue goals they aren't suited for without transparency or feedback, the trust loop breaks. In John's case, the organization wasted time and resources delaying needed change, and he risked his own credibility by trying to fit into a role he wasn't built for. Trust 360 reinforces a shared understanding that growth doesn't mean grabbing titles; it means expanding value.

Alignment Requires Courage and Organizational Maturity

It takes courage to say, "I'm not the right fit," just as it takes maturity for an organization to support that kind of honesty without judgment. Trust 360 cultivates both. It reframes these moments not as weakness, but as wisdom and creates a system where learning becomes continuous rather than corrective.

Tools Are Only as Good as the Trust They Rest On

The tools from Chapter 5, while powerful, can only work when trust is present. A team that uses a Canvas exercise in a low-trust environment will simply play it safe. But in a culture that embraces Trust 360, those same tools become transformative, unlocking alignment not just with goals, but with one another.

Yet alignment is not only about tasks and roles. It reaches deeper into the human experience. Even when people are working in their 20% zone and contributing from their strengths, they cannot sustain peak performance if they feel internally misaligned. True trust-based leadership requires recognizing that people are more than their output—they are whole human beings with values, purpose, and inner balance. This realization led us to explore an often-overlooked dimension of leadership: spiritual balance.

CHAPTER 7

Leadership Spiritual Balance

I once had an administrative staff member who seemed unstoppable. He had a rare ability to anticipate needs, juggle multiple priorities, and take ownership of whatever task landed on his desk. Whenever someone asked for help, his answer was always yes. For a time, it looked like a dream. He made the office run smoothly and freed the rest of us to focus on higher-level work.

But beneath the surface, the cost was mounting. He never paused to check his own capacity or to set boundaries. He worked long hours, quietly carrying more than anyone realized. Eventually, the weight became too much. Deadlines began to slip, details were missed, and cracks appeared in what had once been seamless operations. What looked like reliability was, in truth, unsustainable overextension.

Watching him struggle was a sobering reminder: even the most capable, committed people cannot thrive when they are out of balance. Burnout is not only about workload—it's about losing the connection between one's work, one's values, and one's own well-being. That lesson became a turning point in how I thought about leadership.

Why Balance Matters

In the dynamic world of leadership, the pursuit of balance is often confined to work-life integration or decision-making processes. However, there exists a deeper dimension that leaders must address: the spiritual and psychological balance of their team members. This balance is not merely about religious or spiritual beliefs, but about aligning actions with values, purpose, and inner peace. When individuals feel they have strayed from this alignment, either by wrongdoing against others or failing to adhere to their own moral compass, they can become trapped in a cycle of guilt, self-doubt, and diminished effectiveness. Leaders who recognize and facilitate the restoration of this balance unlock not only the potential for personal growth but also the emergence of a stronger, more cohesive team.

The absence of spiritual balance often manifests as decreased morale and disengagement. These effects ripple outward, influencing team dynamics, productivity, and overall organizational health. Leaders who proactively address these imbalances demonstrate a deeper commitment to their team's well-being, fostering trust and loyalty. By nurturing this balance, leaders pave the way for individuals to reconnect with their sense of purpose, enabling them to contribute more effectively both professionally and personally.

This chapter explores the transformative power of leadership in helping team members navigate their internal struggles, emphasizing the importance of creating environments that encourage healing, redemption, and growth.

The Role of Leadership in Spiritual Reconciliation

Leadership extends beyond managing tasks and achieving goals. At its core, leadership involves guiding individuals toward becoming their best selves. When a person feels they have done wrong, it can create an emotional and psychological rift that hinders their ability to contribute effectively. Leaders have a unique opportunity to act as facilitators of reconciliation, helping individuals reconcile their actions with their inner values. By fostering an environment of trust, accountability, and compassion, leaders can create pathways for individuals to address their inner conflicts and emerge stronger. This not only benefits the individual but also enhances the collective strength and resilience of the organization.

The essence of reconciliation lies in creating spaces for open communication. When leaders actively listen and validate the experiences of their team members, they build bridges of trust that encourage openness. This environment allows individuals to admit mistakes without fear of reprisal, shifting the focus from blame to growth. Leaders who embody humility and understanding inspire their teams to do the same, cultivating a culture of empathy and shared accountability.

Moreover, leadership in this context requires a balance of firmness and empathy. While accountability is vital, it must be accompanied by compassion to ensure that individuals feel supported rather than judged. By modeling this approach, leaders set the tone for a workplace that values growth over perfection, fostering resilience and innovation.

Recognizing the Signs of Inner Conflict

People who feel they have done something wrong often exhibit signs of inner turmoil, though these signs may not always be overt. They might withdraw from team interactions, exhibit defensiveness when approached, or overcompensate by taking on excessive workloads. These behaviors, though varied, stem from an unresolved sense of guilt or failure. As a leader, the key lies in recognizing these patterns with empathy and a willingness to engage. Rather than focusing solely on performance metrics, leaders must tune into the emotional and psychological well-being of their team members, creating space for honest dialogue and understanding.

Recognizing inner conflict requires both observation and intuition. Leaders should look beyond surface behaviors to identify underlying issues that may be affecting performance or morale. For instance, sudden changes in behavior, such as uncharacteristic silence or excessive eagerness to please, may indicate unresolved guilt or fear. By approaching these situations with curiosity rather than judgment, leaders can uncover the root causes of the conflict and provide meaningful support.

It's also important for leaders to cultivate emotional intelligence. By being attuned to the emotional undercurrents within their teams, they can address issues before they escalate. Regular check-ins, anonymous surveys, and open-door policies are practical tools that can help leaders stay connected to their team's emotional health.

The Transformative Power of Doing Good

One of the most effective ways to help individuals regain their spiritual and psychological balance is by giving them the opportunity to do good. Positive actions serve as a form of redemption, enabling individuals to realign with their values and purpose. Leaders can guide team members toward meaningful contributions that have tangible impacts, whether through mentorship roles, community service initiatives, or projects that leverage their unique strengths. When people see the positive outcomes of their efforts, it reaffirms their sense of worth and capacity to make amends, fostering both personal healing and a renewed commitment to the organization's mission.

Doing good is not limited to grand gestures; even small acts of kindness or meaningful contributions can have a profound impact. For example, involving individuals in mentoring junior team members or spearheading a charitable initiative can help them reconnect with their sense of purpose. These activities provide a dual benefit: they help the individual feel valued and contribute positively to the team or community.

Leaders play a crucial role in identifying opportunities that align with an individual's skills and interests. By doing so, they ensure that the experience is both meaningful and impactful. This alignment not only aids in personal growth but also strengthens the individual's commitment to the organization's goals. Over time, these positive experiences can help individuals rebuild their confidence and regain their sense of balance.

Steps to Foster Spiritual Psychological Balance

1. **Acknowledge the wrong:** Open and non-judgmental communication is the foundation of reconciliation. Leaders must create safe spaces where individuals can acknowledge their mistakes without fear of excessive judgment. This acknowledgment is the first step toward healing. By addressing mistakes openly, leaders send a message that growth and redemption are valued over perfection.

2. **Encourage accountability:** Accountability is essential for growth. Leaders can guide individuals to take responsibility for their actions in a constructive manner, ensuring that this process leads to learning rather than self-punishment. Accountability should be framed as an opportunity for growth, where individuals are encouraged to reflect on their actions and identify steps for improvement.

3. **Offer redemption opportunities:** Providing opportunities for positive action helps individuals rebuild their confidence and

align their actions with their values. Assigning tasks that allow them to make meaningful contributions is a powerful way to support this evolution. These opportunities should be tailored to the individual's strengths, ensuring that they feel capable and supported throughout the process.

4. **Promote reflection and growth:** Encouraging practices such as journaling, mentorship, or reflective discussions helps individuals process their experiences and extract valuable lessons. These activities nurture resilience and personal insight. Leaders can facilitate these practices by providing time and resources, as well as sharing their own experiences to inspire openness.

5. **Celebrate progress:** Recognizing and celebrating efforts to restore balance reinforces positive behavior and fosters a culture of growth and encouragement within the organization. Leaders should acknowledge both small and significant milestones, using these moments to highlight the value of perseverance and growth.

Case Studies

In the early stages of our company's development, we were learning by doing. Inevitably, we made some poor decisions that upset those we brought on board or created internal rifts. One striking example involved hiring an individual with a prestigious track record to help develop our business. Despite a year of effort, we hadn't moved the needle. We either failed to provide the necessary support for that individual or didn't fully recognize his strengths, expecting him to fulfill an all-encompassing role. This left both the individual disappointed and our company without the results we had hoped for. Both the individual and the company were out of balance.

However, by maintaining our relationship with this individual even after he moved on to another job, we began to restore balance. Over time, this mutual support led to him helping us grow our business while we supported his new assignments. This reconnection created a perfect example of reestablishing balance. It required leadership to recognize that the issue was one of imbalance and that addressing it could bring significant benefits. Too often, relationships dissolve without addressing the root causes of the imbalance, which is a missed opportunity for growth and healing.

In another instance, we brought on an employee with exceptional intellectual capabilities and an impressive pedigree. We were fortunate to attract such talent. However, over time, it became clear that this individual's superiority created imbalances in team dynamics and certain activities. As we were still in a period of organizational learning, this imbalance eventually led to the individual leaving our company to work for one of our clients. Both parties—the individual and the company—felt a sense of loss over how the situation unfolded.

Despite this, we maintained a strong relationship with the individual after their departure. Eventually, balance was restored as the individual rose to lead our client's organization, and we became their trusted partner. This "win-win-win" scenario exemplifies the immense benefits of restoring balance, even after initial challenges. Through these experiences, we learned that addressing imbalances with intentionality and care can lead to transformative outcomes for all involved.

The Ripple Effect on the Organization

When individuals regain their spiritual and psychological balance, the benefits extend far beyond personal well-being. Restored individuals bring renewed energy, focus, and positivity to their teams. They are better equipped to collaborate, innovate, and contribute to organizational goals.

Moreover, when leaders prioritize balance and reconciliation, they set a powerful example for the entire organization, fostering a culture of trust, empathy, and resilience. This ripple effect ultimately strengthens the organization's foundation, making it more adaptive and cohesive.

Organizations that invest in the spiritual balance of their teams often see improvements in overall morale, productivity, and retention rates. By addressing imbalances and promoting growth, leaders create environments where individuals feel valued and motivated. This not only enhances individual performance but also strengthens the collective capacity of the organization to navigate challenges and seize opportunities.

Conclusion: Leadership as a Catalyst for Healing

Leadership is not merely about driving results; it is about unlocking potential—in people, teams, and organizations. By recognizing and addressing the spiritual and psychological imbalances of team members, leaders can act as catalysts for profound healing and growth. In doing so, they nurture a culture where individuals feel valued, empowered, and whole. This balance is not only essential for personal fulfillment but also for achieving the collective greatness of the organization.

Leaders who embrace this role serve as beacons of hope and inspiration, demonstrating that mistakes and setbacks are not the end but rather opportunities for growth and redemption. By fostering spiritual psychological balance, leaders not only support individuals but also elevate their organizations to new heights of success and cohesion.

The balance leaders cultivate within their teams does not stop at the organizational boundary. When trust, healing, and alignment are present internally, they radiate outward, shaping how we engage with clients, partners, and communities. In essence, the same principles that restore wholeness within a team become the foundation for building credibility and long-lasting relationships outside the organization. Business development, then, is not a detached function driven by numbers and proposals; it is an extension of trust-based leadership. This recognition set the stage for my next discovery: how trust became the cornerstone of growth and opportunity in business development.

In Japanese culture, there is a deep value placed on *wa*—harmony—or what some also describe through the concept of *ha*, the respectful balance between individuals and the group. Harmony is not the absence of conflict, but the presence of mutual respect, trust, and alignment. When leaders create this kind of balance within their organizations, it naturally extends outward, shaping how the organization shows up in its external relationships. Much like in Japanese society, where harmony is seen as a foundation for collective progress, in business development, trust and alignment serve as the invisible threads that bind partnerships together.

I first realized this connection during a client meeting years ago. We had spent weeks preparing a proposal that highlighted every technical detail of our capabilities. Yet when we sat down with the client, the conversation barely touched the proposal. Instead, they wanted to know who we were, how we treated our people, and whether we could be trusted to stand by them when challenges arose. In that moment, it became clear: the balance and trust we fostered inside our organization would either open or close the doors of opportunity outside of it. Business development wasn't just about proposals—it was about relationships, credibility, and character. That's where the next chapter of my leadership journey began.

CHAPTER 8

Business Development Through RCC

The Role of Trust in Business Development

Business development is fundamentally built on trust. No matter how great your service, product, or expertise is, if a client doesn't know you, they are unlikely to buy from you. It is especially true for small businesses, where visibility and reputation take time to establish. Many companies believe that winning contracts is simply about submitting strong proposals with competitive pricing, but the reality is far more complex. Trust is the invisible currency that determines success in business development.

When I started my business over twenty years ago, I had a simple approach: if we saw a Request for Proposal (RFP) that aligned with our expertise, we would go after it. These requests were publicly advertised, and the scope of work often matched what we did daily. It seemed like a perfect opportunity to showcase our technical capability and win contracts. We invested time and resources into writing detailed proposals, ensuring we met all the requirements.

Yet, despite our efforts, we kept losing. Our proposals were rejected, often with the same frustrating evaluation: technically unacceptable. This confused us. The work described in the RFP was something we had done before, and we were confident in our ability to execute. We had the qualifications, experience, and resources, so why were we not even making it past the first round?

After multiple losses, we began to analyze what was happening. It wasn't our pricing, and it wasn't that we lacked the capability. The problem was much deeper: we didn't know the client. We had submitted proposals to organizations where we had no prior engagement, no established relationship, and no trust. To the decision-makers, we were just another unknown bidder. They had no reason to choose us over a competitor they already knew.

Looking back, the mistake seems obvious, but at the time, we thought our expertise would speak for itself. We had no idea that relationships mattered just as much—if not more—than technical qualifications. We were submitting proposals blindly, expecting that a well-written response would be enough to win the business. It wasn't.

Recognizing our lack of client relationships, we decided to approach things differently. Instead of going in alone, we partnered with another company that claimed to have strong connections with the client. Their relationship, we assumed, would bridge the trust gap and increase our chances of winning.

With this new strategy in mind, we dedicated four weeks to preparing a large, detailed proposal. Our teaming partner provided input, and we structured our approach based on the methodology in which we were experts. This time, we were certain we had done everything right.

Three months later, the result was the same: a loss. But this time, the reason was even more frustrating: our technical approach was completely off.

How was this possible? Didn't our partner know the client? Yes, but only at a surface level. They were familiar with the organization but had no real relationship with the actual decision-makers within the buying group. Their connection wasn't strong enough to influence the outcome.

This was a harsh but necessary lesson. Not only did we lack a relationship with the client, but we also failed to properly vet our teaming partner. We had assumed their relationships were meaningful and relevant, but they weren't. They knew of the client, but they did not know the people making the purchasing decision. That was the difference between success and failure.

These repeated failures forced us to rethink our approach. Winning contracts wasn't just about proving our expertise; it was about building trust long before an RFP was ever released. We needed a new strategy that didn't rely solely on technical capability but instead focused on establishing meaningful Relationships, Capability, and Credibility (RCC).

We realized that without a strong "R" for Relationship, we would never be able to effectively showcase our "C" for Capability or establish the "C" for Credibility. Clients needed to know us, trust us, and believe in our ability to deliver.

This chapter explores how we improved our business development approach by integrating RCC into our strategy. By focusing on Relationships, Capability, and Credibility, we learned how to position ourselves for success by building trust first and proving value second.

Now, let's break down each element of RCC and how it plays a critical role in business growth.

Relationships: The Foundation of Business Development

Relationships are the foundation of trust in business. Without a relationship, you are just another name in the pile of bidders. Key decision-makers need to know and trust you before you ever submit a proposal. A strong relationship provides insight into the client's challenges, priorities, and expectations—insights that can't be found in an RFP document.

Building relationships requires more than just networking—it's about adding value before you ask for anything in return. This can be done through industry engagement, thought leadership, and genuinely helping potential clients solve problems before contracts are on the table. For example, attending industry conferences, hosting webinars, or providing educational resources can position you as a trusted advisor in your field. Strong relationships ensure that when a need arises, you're already seen as a reliable option.

Another aspect of relationship-building is consistency and follow-through. Too often, businesses make initial connections but fail to nurture them over time. Staying engaged, checking in, and offering help without immediate expectations builds genuine rapport. Clients remember who was there when they didn't need anything. Those are the partners they turn to when they do.

Capability: Demonstrating Expertise and Excellence

Capability is the backbone of a business's ability to deliver results. It's not enough to have experience. You need to continuously develop and prove that your expertise remains at the cutting edge. Clients want to know that you not only understand their needs but that you have the skills and methodologies to execute successfully.

One of the biggest mistakes small businesses make is assuming that capability alone is enough to win contracts. Being good at what you do isn't a differentiator; you must prove that you can apply your capability to the client's specific challenges. Capability must be showcased in a way that aligns with business development efforts.

Demonstrating capability involves more than listing qualifications. It's about providing evidence of success through project results, innovation, and industry contributions. It can be done through case studies, performance metrics, and ongoing professional development. Clients are more likely to engage with a business that shows proof of concept rather than just stating expertise.

Additionally, capability isn't static. Industries evolve, and so should businesses. Investing in professional development, staying ahead of industry trends, and adopting new technologies demonstrate a commitment to excellence. Clients want partners who don't just meet the standard but set the standard.

Credibility: Establishing Trust and Authority

Credibility is earned over time through consistent performance, transparency, and ethical business practices. It's not just about what you say you can do; it's about what others know you can do. A company with a strong track record of delivering results builds credibility that makes clients feel confident in their decision to work with them.

Credibility also plays a crucial role in how businesses navigate competition. When clients trust you, they are more willing to listen, even when competitors undercut pricing. They recognize that working with a credible partner reduces risk and ensures quality outcomes. Without credibility, even the best proposal can feel like an empty promise.

Establishing credibility requires proof of past success. Case studies, testimonials, and references from satisfied clients go a long way in demonstrating credibility. Additionally, thought leadership, such as publishing articles, speaking at industry events, or participating in advisory boards, further cements an organization's authority in its field. The more visible and credible you are, the easier it becomes to earn a client's trust.

Another key element of credibility is transparency. Clients appreciate honesty about challenges, realistic expectations, and clear communication. Businesses that acknowledge potential risks upfront and proactively address concerns build trust far faster than those that overpromise and underdeliver.

Integrating RCC into Business Development Strategies

Understanding RCC is one thing; applying it effectively is another. Successful business development requires an intentional approach to integrating Relationships, Capability, and Credibility into a cohesive strategy. This means engaging with potential clients well before an RFP is published, nurturing relationships over time, and ensuring your capability and credibility are visible in the industry. It also means carefully selecting and vetting partners to ensure they bring real value to the table. A well-executed RCC strategy leads to smoother contract negotiations, stronger partnerships, and higher long-term success rates.

A strong RCC approach also allows businesses to pre-position themselves before opportunities arise. Instead of reacting to RFPs, businesses should be engaging with potential clients, understanding their challenges, and building trust ahead of time. When opportunities finally emerge, businesses that have invested in RCC are already positioned as trusted, go-to partners.

Another key element of integrating RCC is aligning it with the company's overall marketing, branding, and sales strategy. Business development is not a separate function—it is intertwined with how a company presents itself to the world. A business that is consistently engaging, delivering high-quality work, and demonstrating thought leadership will naturally attract new opportunities.

At its core, business development is about trust. When clients trust you, they don't just award contracts; they become long-term partners. RCC is not just a strategy; it's a mindset that transforms how we approach growth and leadership.

Integrating RCC into leadership means emphasizing relationship-building, ethical decision-making, and continuous learning. It ensures that trust is built not just with clients, but within your organization as well. Leaders who foster an RCC-driven culture encourage their teams to prioritize long-term partnerships over short-term wins, maintain integrity in negotiations, and continuously improve their skill sets.

A trust-based leadership approach built on RCC also helps businesses navigate challenges more effectively. When relationships are strong, credibility is established, and capability is proven, businesses become resilient. Clients turn to trusted partners in times of uncertainty, and companies with strong RCC foundations find themselves in a position of stability even in turbulent markets.

By applying these principles, we've learned how to turn losses into lessons, challenges into opportunities, and trust into growth. RCC is not just about winning business—it's about leading with integrity, proving value, and building a legacy of success.

The more our company grew, the clearer it became that winning business was only the first step. Strong relationships, demonstrated capability, and established credibility brought clients to the table, but sustaining those partnerships required something deeper. Trust could open doors, but keeping them open demanded discipline, structure, and a way to prove—day after day—that we could deliver on what we promised. That's when I realized that trust and process are inseparable: one inspires belief, the other sustains it.

Continuous Process Improvement (CPI) became the framework through which we translated RCC into consistent performance. Relationships created the foundation, credibility anchored confidence, and capability proved itself not just in words but in measurable results. Internally, CPI gave our teams a shared language and rhythm, a way to turn good intentions into lasting outcomes. Externally, it reassured clients that our promises were backed by systems designed to endure.

Yet I also discovered how fragile this balance can be. In one hospital system we partnered with, the trust we worked so hard to build began to crumble under outside pressures. What started as a story of excitement and progress turned into a sobering reminder: when trust falters, the cost is not only organizational, but also deeply human.

CHAPTER 9

Trust-Based Leadership and Continuous Process Improvement

An essential aspect of trust-based leadership that significantly impacts organizational success is its relationship with CPI. This chapter explores how foundational trust established through leadership practices is crucial for implementing and sustaining improvement efforts. Without trust, even the most promising strategies will falter. With it, organizations unlock the potential for meaningful, sustainable transformation.

A Leadership Moment That Changed Me

Several years ago, our company was hired to develop and implement a CPI program for a mid-sized hospital system. It was a promising engagement, one we approached with thoughtful planning, high energy, and a genuine belief that we could help the system improve the way it delivered care.

After weeks of detailed contract negotiations and collaborative discussions, we formally launched the program using our phased engagement model. Senior leadership at the hospital was deeply committed. They demonstrated this by creating a new leadership role—the Vice President of Quality and Process Improvement—and appointing a sharp, mission-driven leader to fill it. She quickly hired a small team that we would train and mentor to become the hospital's internal CPI experts. The intent was clear: this wasn't just a consulting contract; this was a long-term partnership.

In those early months, there was a noticeable buzz throughout the organization. Our team conducted a comprehensive evaluation and designed an implementation roadmap tailored to the hospital's unique culture and challenges. We launched improvement projects across departments and rolled out training programs in multiple hospitals and clinics across the system. You could feel the excitement in the hallways. Front-line staff were engaged, managers were curious, and the VP we worked with was fully invested. I vividly remember walking into one of the hospitals and seeing nurses gathered around a process map, adding Post-its and debating bottlenecks. We were making progress, and more importantly, we were building trust.

But that momentum was soon challenged by forces beyond our control.

In 2009 and 2010, sweeping U.S. healthcare reforms—particularly the Affordable Care Act—began to fundamentally alter the landscape for hospitals nationwide. While the reforms were rooted in noble goals, such as expanding access and reducing systemic costs, they brought tremendous strain to small and mid-sized healthcare systems. Reimbursement structures changed abruptly. Penalties were introduced for hospital readmissions. Operating margins were squeezed, and regulatory pressures increased. Larger health systems with greater financial reserves could adapt more easily, but for mid-sized providers like the one we were supporting, the pressure was immense.

Leadership at the hospital system found itself in survival mode. Suddenly, every expense was scrutinized. Cost containment became the dominant conversation. Departments were asked to identify redundancies and trim budgets quickly. The trust we had built—the foundation upon which all CPI efforts depend—began to falter.

Almost overnight, the narrative around our work shifted, not because of anything we had done differently, but because the external environment had fundamentally changed. What had once been embraced as a vehicle for innovation, collaboration, and staff empowerment was now being viewed through a lens of skepticism and fear. Staff began whispering in hallways and questioning in meetings whether CPI was truly about improvement, or if it was just a covert strategy to identify inefficiencies for the sole purpose of cutting jobs. The very tools and techniques we had introduced to streamline workflows and elevate patient care were now being seen as instruments of downsizing.

This shift wasn't just among front-line staff; it reached middle managers and even some senior leaders who had once championed the program. As layoffs began across departments, the mood darkened. Anxiety grew. Employees became guarded, reluctant to participate in improvement workshops, and hesitant to speak candidly. Fear spread quickly, and with it, the psychological safety that had taken months to cultivate began to disappear. Trust—something we had worked tirelessly to build through transparency, engagement, and shared victories—began to erode, not in one dramatic moment, but in a slow and steady unraveling that none of us could stop.

As the president of my company and the leader of this engagement, I felt the weight of it all. My team had poured itself into this work. They had built relationships, trained staff, and delivered measurable early wins. And now I had to find a way to keep them motivated in an environment where we were no longer seen as partners, but as threats.

I held one-on-one conversations with each member of the consulting team, not only to manage the project but also to boost morale. I reminded them why we started, what we had accomplished, and the value we were still bringing. But I could see the toll it was taking. When your presence causes fear instead of trust, it's a signal that the system is no longer ready to improve. It was disheartening. And for me, it was personal.

The breaking point came when the hospital CEO made the painful but, in their view, necessary decision to cut nursing staff. That decision shifted the perception of leadership across the organization. It no longer felt like this was a place fighting to improve; it felt like a place trying to survive. The CPI program became a casualty of that shift. The same VP who had once inspired her staff and partnered so closely with us was now tasked with dismantling her own team. One by one, the internal CPI staff we had trained were let go.

Eventually, we exited, not because our work failed or the methodology was flawed, but because the trust that CPI needs to function had vanished. In its place was fear, fatigue, and retrenchment.

This experience taught me one of the most important lessons of my career: **No amount of process improvement can succeed in an environment where trust has been broken.** Without trust, even the most sophisticated tools and techniques become irrelevant. Without trust, communication dries up, collaboration dissolves, and decisions are made out of fear rather than purpose.

As a leader, I walked away from this engagement with a deep respect for the fragility of trust and the power it holds over everything we try to do in organizations. And I came to understand that trust must be protected, not just built. Because when it is lost, the cost is more than financial. The cost is human.

The Foundation of Trust for Improvement Initiatives

Trust is not a luxury in continuous improvement—it is a requirement. It serves as the invisible key that unlocks access to the processes, people, and data needed to drive transformation. No matter how compelling the business case for change, or how proven the methodology, improvement initiatives cannot take root in an environment where trust does not exist.

A useful metaphor to frame this truth is the idea of inviting someone into your home. You may admire or respect them from a distance, but without trust, you won't hand them the keys or allow them to examine your most personal spaces. The same principle applies to organizations. Leaders and staff alike will not open their operations or themselves to scrutiny and change unless they feel secure in the motives, integrity, and competence of those proposing the improvement.

This dynamic is even more pronounced in engagements that involve external consultants or cross-functional teams. Allowing outsiders to review operations and make recommendations requires a leap of faith. It often involves revealing inefficiencies, vulnerabilities, or cultural dysfunctions that organizations may not even admit to internally. Without a strong foundation of trust, even the act of identifying problems can feel threatening.

Our experience working with a mid-sized hospital system made this reality painfully clear. In the beginning, trust was earned through intentional effort—structured engagement, a transparent plan, deep listening, and alignment with leadership. Staff participation was strong, and enthusiasm grew quickly. But as external pressures from healthcare reform mounted, that trust evaporated. Suddenly, our presence was no longer seen as helpful but suspicious. Improvement work, once welcomed as a force for good, was perceived as a precursor to cuts and layoffs. The fear overwhelmed the trust, and without trust, we had no path forward.

This experience revealed a critical insight: **trust is not a byproduct of improvement—it is a prerequisite.**

Leaders who want to enable CPI must first create the conditions in which trust can exist and thrive. This doesn't happen passively. It requires conscious actions that signal empathy, respect, and partnership from the very beginning.

Building Trust Before Improvement Begins

Establishing trust must precede any formal improvement effort. It does not happen automatically and cannot be assumed. Instead, it requires deliberate and consistent actions that signal respect, safety, and shared purpose. The following are critical practices that leaders and consultants must embrace to lay a strong trust foundation before launching any CPI initiative:

- **Demonstrating alignment with the organization's mission and values**

    Before suggesting changes or offering solutions, leaders must show that they understand and respect the mission that drives the organization. This includes speaking the language of the organization, referencing its stated values, and honoring its purpose-driven culture. When stakeholders see that you are not there to impose a generic solution but to support their unique goals, a foundation of trust begins to form. It tells them: *We are here to help you fulfill your mission—not disrupt it.*

- **Respecting the lived experience of front-line employees**

    Too often, improvement initiatives are designed in boardrooms and implemented without meaningful engagement from those doing the actual work. Trust is built when employees feel seen and heard, when their expertise is acknowledged, and their input is actively solicited. This means engaging with humility, asking more questions than offering answers, and validating the challenges they've faced. When people realize you're not there to critique their performance but to work alongside them, they begin to lower their guard.

- **Practicing radical transparency with leadership and staff alike**

  Transparency is one of the fastest ways to build or destroy trust. Leaders must be transparent about the objectives of the improvement initiative, including how success will be measured, the associated risks, and the unknowns. This includes being candid about constraints, timelines, and the potential impacts of change. When people understand *why* something is being done and *how* decisions are made, they are more likely to engage, even if the answers are difficult.

- **Acknowledging uncertainty and vulnerability, especially in times of change**

  Trust isn't only built through strength; it's also built through vulnerability. Leaders who admit what they don't know, who acknowledge the fears and concerns of their teams, and who communicate empathy in uncertain moments earn deeper loyalty and connection. In CPI work, acknowledging that "we don't have all the answers yet" or "this will likely be difficult at first" creates a climate of authenticity. It shows that improvement is shared, not a scripted solution imposed from above.

These practices do more than set the tone for a project—they create the conditions in which trust can take root and grow. Without this foundation, even the best-designed CPI programs risk becoming performative exercises, resented rather than embraced. With it, improvement becomes a shared act of purpose, resilience, and transformation.

Demonstrating alignment with the organization's mission and values

Respecting the lived experience of front-line employees

Practicing radical transparency with leadership and staff alike

Acknowledging uncertainty and vulnerability, especially in times of change

Enabling Continuous Process Improvement

Once a foundation of trust is established, it creates the conditions in which CPI can truly take hold. Trust transforms improvement from a compliance exercise into a participatory culture, where people are not just willing but *eager* to find better ways of working.

In organizations where trust is present, employees feel safe to identify inefficiencies, speak openly about obstacles, and take ownership of solutions. They are not paralyzed by fear of blame or retribution. Instead, they are encouraged to think critically, take initiative, and view change not as a disruption but as an opportunity. This psychological safety—the belief that one can contribute ideas, raise concerns, or admit mistakes without negative consequences—is one of the most powerful enablers of innovation.

In contrast, environments that lack trust tend to breed defensiveness, silence, and resistance. Employees may nod along in meetings but remain disengaged. Problems are hidden or minimized, and improvement efforts are met with skepticism or avoidance. Without trust, CPI initiatives stall—not because the tools are wrong, but because the human system around them is frozen.

The Role of Trust-Based Leadership

Trust-based leadership is the engine that drives continuous improvement forward. It empowers teams to act, adapt, and contribute without fear, turning improvement into a shared endeavor rather than a top-down mandate. Leaders who lead with trust model vulnerability, show up consistently, and foster dialogue across all levels of the organization.

Here's how trust-based leadership activates and sustains CPI:

Speak Truth to Power

In a trusted environment, employees feel empowered to share what's really going on, not just what leadership wants to hear. This is critical for uncovering systemic issues that often remain hidden in low-trust cultures. Staff must feel empowered to raise red flags, challenge ineffective practices, or question long-standing routines without fear of retaliation. Trust-based leaders respond with curiosity, not defensiveness. They make it safe to say, "This isn't working," and they reward honesty over harmony. As a result, root causes can be surfaced and addressed, rather than covered up.

Take Intelligent Risks

Continuous improvement requires experimentation. Whether it's piloting a new patient discharge protocol or adjusting a supply chain workflow, the process involves trial and error. In a high-trust environment, teams are encouraged to take calculated risks, explore alternatives, and learn from failure. Leaders help establish the boundary between acceptable experimentation and reckless behavior, and they reinforce that failing in the pursuit of better is not a liability, but a learning opportunity. This creates a climate where innovation becomes part of daily work, not just a one-time initiative.

Collaborate Across Boundaries

Trust doesn't stop at the individual level—it must extend across teams, departments, and hierarchies. In many organizations, silos block improvement efforts, as people withhold information, protect turf, or mistrust each other's motives. Trust-based leadership fosters cross-functional respect and transparency. Leaders model open communication, create forums for interdisciplinary dialogue, and reinforce shared goals. When teams trust each other, they're more likely to share best practices, pool resources, and align around common metrics, dramatically accelerating the pace and scale of improvement.

Sustain Momentum

CPI is not a sprint; it's a long-distance discipline. Sustaining momentum requires more than dashboards and check-ins; it requires emotional commitment. In environments of trust, people are more willing to stay engaged through setbacks, delays, and resistance. They feel part of something bigger than their individual role. Trust-based leaders cultivate this commitment by celebrating small wins, recognizing effort as well as outcomes, and staying personally involved, not just at kickoff, but throughout the improvement process. They reinforce a shared belief that the work matters and that progress, even if slow, is worth continuing.

The Consultant's Challenge: Navigating Vulnerability

For clients and potential clients, the decision to bring in an external partner to lead or support process improvement is not simply a technical or financial decision—it is a deeply relational one. Allowing someone from the outside to examine internal operations, sit in team meetings, review workflows, and ask probing questions is an act of organizational vulnerability. It is an invitation into sacred space.

Clients need to know that those entering that space will do so with competence, care, and discretion.

They must believe that the consultants:

- Understand the complexities of their environment
- Are there to enable—not control—the change process
- Will leave the organization stronger, not more exposed

In the story of the mid-sized hospital system, we experienced firsthand what happens when that trust is compromised—not because of malintent, but because broader forces of fear and uncertainty overtook the narrative. CPI became misidentified as a threat, and the space we had been welcomed into was suddenly closed off. The lesson was clear: **The permission to lead change can be revoked the moment trust is lost.**

CPI in a High-Trust Culture

Organizations that sustain trust—especially during uncertainty—experience a different trajectory. In these environments:

- Employees volunteer to participate in Kaizen events and improvement teams.
- Leaders actively seek feedback, even when it challenges the status quo.
- Front-line staff initiate small daily improvements without waiting for approval.
- Metrics are used not as punishment, but as tools for learning and dialogue.

These organizations don't just *do* CPI—they *live* it. Improvement becomes embedded in how they think, behave, and grow.

Building Trust with Clients for Continuous Improvement

Trust with clients is not a transactional checkbox; it is a strategic relationship, nurtured over time, and essential to the success of any continuous improvement engagement. CPI requires clients to open up the inner workings of their organization: their systems, workflows, and, more vulnerably, their people. This level of transparency and access demands a foundation of trust that goes beyond contractual obligations. It requires the client to believe that their partner's intent is aligned with their mission, that their methods are sound, and that their presence will ultimately leave the organization stronger than it was before.

What makes CPI engagements unique is that they are inherently immersive. Unlike traditional consulting that delivers a report or solution set at arm's length, CPI work unfolds within the organization itself. It touches cross-functional teams, spans from executive boardrooms to front-line operations, and asks for introspection, experimentation, and change. The clients we work with must feel safe inviting us into this process. Without that safety and trust, the engagement becomes fragile, misunderstood, or even resented.

The first signal of trust begins with transparency. From the earliest conversations, it's essential to be open and honest—not only about what we plan to do, but also how we intend to do it and why we believe it matters. Clients need to understand the logic behind our methods, the tools we use, and the pathways through which recommendations are made. Equally important is being candid about what we don't know, acknowledging risks, limitations, and the areas where we will need their help. Transparency says, *We are not here to operate in the shadows. We are here to build something with you, not for you.* And that message is essential to reducing skepticism and surfacing buy-in.

Next comes the practice of listening deeply. Before introducing change, we must understand the context in which it will exist. And that understanding cannot come solely from executive briefings or strategic documents. It must come from the voices of those who keep the organization running each day—nurses, technicians, schedulers, analysts, and line managers. Listening, when done well, becomes a form of respect. It demonstrates that we do not see the organization as broken, but as full of people who care, who are capable, and who deserve to be part of shaping the future. When clients see that we truly understand their culture, constraints, and aspirations, trust deepens. They begin to believe, not just that we know what we're doing, but that we know who they are.

Of course, belief alone is not enough. Early in a CPI engagement, we must show tangible progress. This is where the importance of quick wins becomes critical. Small, visible successes—such as reducing unnecessary process steps, improving patient handoffs, or redesigning supply chains—build momentum and reduce resistance. Quick wins are not about checking a box; they are about creating proof that the process works. These early victories send a powerful message: *This is not theory. This is action. And it's working.* For organizations that have experienced failed change efforts in the past, these early results can be the difference between continued hesitation and full engagement.

At the heart of all of this is inclusion. Continuous improvement cannot be imposed from the top down; it must be co-created across every level of the organization. True trust is built when employees feel that they are part of the process, not subject to it. This means more than attending meetings or filling out surveys. It means involving staff in mapping their own processes, inviting their ideas for improvement, and trusting them to test and implement solutions. When people feel that they have agency, they develop ownership. And with ownership comes pride and commitment that outlasts any formal engagement.

Finally, one of the most powerful ways to build lasting trust with clients is by sustaining the improvements made. Many organizations have undergone waves of change—initiatives that started with energy but faded due to leadership turnover, shifting priorities, or a lack of follow-through. This breeds cynicism. To counter this, we must help clients institutionalize change: embedding new practices into standard procedures, training internal teams to maintain momentum, and setting up performance tracking to monitor progress over time. When clients see that improvements are not only real but resilient, their confidence in the process and in the partnership solidifies.

Ultimately, trust with clients is not something we earn once and carry forward indefinitely. It is something we renew through every action, every conversation, and every result. When trust is strong, CPI becomes more than a project; it becomes a cultural transformation. Clients stop seeing consultants as outsiders and start seeing them as allies. Together, they build something that lasts.

Trust is not a soft skill; it is the backbone of every successful improvement initiative. Without trust, the best methodologies will be misunderstood, the best strategies resisted, and the best intentions questioned. But when trust is present—when it is built deliberately, nurtured consistently, and protected as a shared value—continuous process improvement becomes not only possible, but transformational.

Trust-based leadership creates the conditions where people speak honestly, take meaningful risks, and collaborate across boundaries. It gives teams the confidence to examine what isn't working and the courage to try something better. And it allows clients to open their organizations to external partners without fear, knowing that what's being built together is rooted in care, capability, and commitment.

The lesson is clear: improvement doesn't begin with tools; it begins with trust. And trust isn't a one-time decision; it's a continuous process in itself. In every engagement and organization, trust is what determines whether improvement takes hold or quietly slips away.

But trust is never static. What sustains it in one era may not be enough in the next. As new generations enter the workforce, they bring with them different expectations shaped by technology, global events, and shifting cultural norms. Their views on work, authority, and meaning don't just add variety; they fundamentally challenge how organizations operate.

The question every leader must now face is this: *Can trust-based leadership evolve fast enough to meet the needs of a generation that refuses to settle for business as usual?* I didn't fully grasp the answer until the day we welcomed our first two Gen Z hires—bright, capable, and ready to challenge everything we thought we knew about leadership.

CHAPTER 10

Trust-Based Leadership and New Generations in the Workforce

A s new generations enter the workforce, their expectations and work habits introduce fresh challenges and opportunities for organizational leadership. Known for their agility, digital fluency, and willingness to move swiftly from one job to another, these newer workforce members place a premium on workplace culture, transparency, and trust. In this context, trust-based leadership becomes not just beneficial but essential for attracting, engaging, and retaining talent from these generations.

Earlier this year, we made a deliberate shift in our hiring approach. For the first time, we brought two Gen Z professionals straight out of college into our organization. Both were exceptional, top of their class, highly intelligent, articulate, and full of promise. We saw it as an opportunity to infuse fresh energy into the company, to challenge old patterns with new thinking, and to create a deeper generational balance within our team.

But very quickly, that decision began to challenge us in ways we hadn't fully anticipated.

What stood out wasn't their capability; both were high achievers with strong academic backgrounds. It was how differently they approached work compared to what we were used to. Each exhibited some of the traits often associated with Gen Z: digital fluency, independence, a preference for authentic dialogue, and an emphasis on mental well-being. But they also brought with them very distinct work rhythms. One of them attacked assignments almost immediately, driven by a strong need to complete tasks as soon as they were received. Waiting felt uncomfortable. Starting right away seemed to bring a sense of control and calm. The other took more time to begin, preferring space for thought, perhaps even a bit of healthy procrastination. But what united them was the lack of urgency around external deadlines. Neither was driven by pressure from above. Their motivation came from within, driven by the desire to complete the work on their own terms.

At first, this puzzled our managers. These were not issues of performance, nor were they signs of disengagement. However, our usual leadership tools, structured timelines, defined check-ins, and traditional supervision, weren't producing the same results we had come to expect. Feedback often landed flat. Motivation didn't spike in the usual ways. It became increasingly clear that something deeper was at play. We were encountering a generational shift, not just in expectations but in how work itself is understood and experienced.

Both individuals were operating from a different framework. They wanted ownership of their time. They expected flexibility and autonomy. And they brought with them a new definition of productivity, one that wasn't tethered to a clock or a desk, but to personal alignment and mental clarity. Even their concept of loyalty felt different. It wasn't assumed; it needed to be earned. Not through compensation or hierarchy, but through growth, purpose, and respect.

It was at this point that I returned to a conversation I had with Ronen Aires, an expert who has spent years studying the mindset of younger generations in the workforce. His insights gave shape to what we were witnessing: this generation isn't difficult to manage; they simply cannot be managed the way we have managed before. As he put it, "It's like bringing home a new laptop and trying to install outdated software on it." They are designed differently. And if we don't upgrade our systems, how we lead, how we communicate, how we engage, we'll lose not just their loyalty, but the tremendous potential they carry.

That realization became a turning point. Instead of asking what was wrong with them, we started asking what needed to change in us.

Understanding the Shift: A New Framework for Work

What we experienced with our new Gen Z team members wasn't a failure of onboarding—it was a mirror. A mirror that reflected how much the landscape of work has changed, and how much leadership needs to evolve in response. These individuals weren't simply rejecting the norms we had built over time; they were revealing how irrelevant some of those norms had quietly become.

Younger generations enter the workforce with a different lens. For them, flexibility isn't a perk, it's a baseline expectation. Work isn't something you clock in and out of; it's something that must integrate with your life, values, and identity. The concept of *work-life balance* has morphed into *work-life integration*, especially since the disruptions of the COVID era. Boundaries have blurred, and the workplace is now wherever there is Wi-Fi. That shift alone redefines how leaders must think about presence, accountability, and productivity.

These new employees aren't asking for less responsibility; they're asking for more autonomy. They don't want to be managed; they want to be guided. They don't want annual performance reviews; they want continuous feedback. And they don't want vague promises about "career paths"—they want growth they can feel *now*. As Ronen put it, they're not loyal by default, but if we show them how to grow and help them unlock their potential, they may stay longer than even they planned. In other words, *guide me to my greatness* is the new contract.

It's not about being softer. It's about being smarter. What we're dealing with isn't entitlement, it's evolution. We're not managing resistance to tradition. We're navigating the birth of a new operating model.

Another key dynamic emerging is how Gen Z and Millennials, despite their age gap, often work extremely well together. Their collaboration is grounded in shared values: empathy, adaptability, tech fluency, and a desire to make a meaningful impact. Together, they form a uniquely agile blend of human-centered and tech-powered performance. They're not afraid of ambiguity. They're not bound by hierarchy. And they're not waiting around for permission to innovate.

Of course, their flexibility comes with its own challenges. Many bring side hustles into their professional lives, not out of disloyalty, but out of curiosity, creativity, and a desire to build something of their own. For some, these ventures are expressions of identity. For others, they're backup plans. Either way, leaders need to acknowledge that these pursuits exist and, in some cases, support them, even if doing so means accepting that the employment relationship may someday end because of it.

The organizations that succeed in this new environment are not those that clamp down or impose rigid structure. They are the ones who reexamine and redesign. This means creating decentralized working environments, allowing for flatter hierarchies and more distributed decision-making. It means redefining what leadership looks like: not as command and control, but as clarity and connection.

What we are learning is that this generation is not broken. They are not fragile. They are not difficult. They are simply built for a different world. And to lead them effectively, we must meet them where they are, not where we once were.

Creating a Culture of Trust and Engagement

Once we accepted that we were operating on outdated leadership assumptions, we began asking: *What does a trust-based culture look like for this generation?* What would it mean to build not just a place to work, but a system where people genuinely want to stay, even when every algorithm, recruiter, and personal passion project is pulling them elsewhere?

At its core, trust-based leadership fosters a culture where transparency, respect, and mutual growth are prioritized. For younger generations, that means moving beyond corporate platitudes and into actionable, everyday behaviors that affirm their value.

It starts with radical transparency. Younger employees want to understand how and why decisions are made. They don't expect perfection, but they expect honesty. Leaders who share openly about the business—not just the good news, but also the uncertainties—build credibility. When employees feel included in the conversation, they invest more deeply in the outcome.

Equally important is empowerment and autonomy. This generation thrives when given the freedom to own their work. Micromanagement erodes trust quickly, while autonomy creates space for innovation and confidence. When leaders frame assignments as opportunities rather than tasks, and when they step back without disengaging, Gen Z responds with initiative.

Another vital component is purpose. For this generation, work must mean something. They are deeply attuned to social and environmental issues, and they want to know how their role contributes to a larger mission. When leaders can draw a clear line between a team member's effort and the broader impact it creates, within the organization or beyond, it changes motivation from transactional to intrinsic.

Continuous feedback and growth opportunities are non-negotiable. Gone are the days of annual performance reviews that feel disconnected from real-time development. *This generation wants feedback in motion:* short, honest, respectful check-ins that signal support and opportunity. When paired with visible learning paths and skill-building options, this creates a sense of trajectory, which, in turn, fuels loyalty.

Finally, trust is amplified when we create a sense of belonging. This generation places a high value on psychological safety, inclusion, and diverse perspectives. They expect to be seen as whole people, not just employees. That includes their mental health, cultural background, and personal values. When they feel they can bring their full selves to work, their engagement deepens.

Ronen's concept of reciprocal mentorship reinforces this further: instead of leadership being a one-way transmission of knowledge, it becomes a loop. Older generations offer wisdom, structure, and grounding. Younger generations bring cultural relevance, tech fluency, and fresh thinking. When we stop trying to "fix" them and start learning with them, we build an ecosystem where trust becomes a shared responsibility.

Organizations that lean into this model—flexible, human, open—create not only stronger engagement, but also more sustainable performance. In today's workplace, trust is not a soft ideal. It is the infrastructure for adaptability, innovation, and long-term success.

Leveraging Trust to Reduce Turnover

For all the conversation about Gen Z's lack of loyalty, the truth is more nuanced. This generation is not disloyal by nature; they're simply unwilling to commit to systems that do not recognize their individual growth, values, or potential. Loyalty, for them, is no longer transactional. It is earned, and it is conditional. And when that condition is trust, the return can be profound.

What we've come to understand is that trust isn't just a cultural asset—it's a strategic one. In an era where side hustles, gig work, and self-employment are increasingly viable alternatives, the gravitational pull of traditional employment is weakening. Younger employees know they have options. And with constant exposure to opportunities through LinkedIn, job boards, and peer networks, their sense of mobility is not just imagined; it's real.

Yet when a culture of trust is present, where leadership is transparent, feedback flows, autonomy is respected, and personal growth is supported, those same employees often choose to stay longer than even they expected. They stay not because they have to, but because they're becoming something better in the process. As Ronen described it, "guide me to my greatness" becomes the silent agreement between employer and employee. If an organization helps them evolve, they often return the favor by committing more deeply.

That evolution, however, must be mutual. Trust isn't built through grand gestures; it's built through consistency. It's built when leaders follow through on what they say. When expectations are clear, growth paths are visible, time off is respected, and voices are heard. Trust is reinforced when flexibility is offered not just as a concession, but as a signal that the organization understands the whole person behind the role.

And finally, trust lowers turnover when organizations loosen their grip on hierarchy. Younger employees respond more favorably to decentralized leadership structures—where authority is shared, not hoarded, and where decision-making is distributed closer to where work actually happens. These models may feel chaotic to traditionalists, but they speak directly to the values of agility, ownership, and inclusion that new generations hold dear.

In the end, reducing turnover isn't about creating barriers to exit. It's about making people want to stay. Trust, when woven into the daily experience of work, becomes the quiet force that stabilizes teams, deepens engagement, and turns short-term hires into long-term contributors. In a world of rapid change and endless choice, trust-based leadership remains one of the few constants that can hold people—and organizations—together.

The Leadership Shift That Can't Wait

What began as an experiment in hiring turned into a revelation: the new generation of workers is not here to be assimilated into outdated systems; they're here to challenge them, evolve them, and in many cases, lead us into a better way of working.

We didn't lose these new hires because they lacked talent or work ethic. In fact, they brought intensity, curiosity, and a desire to do meaningful work. What we nearly lost was the opportunity to fully engage them because we hadn't yet updated our leadership operating system. The patterns and expectations we had relied on for years no longer fit. The world had changed, and so had the workforce. The real question was: had our leadership evolved to match?

Trust-based leadership is not a generational trend; it is a foundational shift. It calls us to lead with greater humility, transparency, and curiosity.

It pushes us to replace command-and-control models with relationships built on mutual growth and shared purpose. It dares us to let go of rigid structures in favor of flexible systems where autonomy and accountability coexist.

And perhaps most importantly, it reminds us that leadership is no longer a one-directional act. Today's leaders must be listeners, learners, and co-creators. When we do this well—when we guide rather than dictate, when we mentor rather than manage—we begin to unlock something extraordinary: the kind of workplace where people don't just show up, they light up.

This generation doesn't need to be convinced to care. They care deeply. What they need is a reason to stay and a culture that reflects the trust they are willing to give, if we're wise enough to earn it.

The future of work isn't arriving someday. It's already here, sitting across from us in meetings, waiting on Slack, or quietly delivering their first project. The only question left is whether we'll lead in a way that meets them or miss the moment entirely.

But people aren't the only force redefining leadership. Alongside the rise of new generations comes another equally disruptive shift—technology. Artificial intelligence is no longer a distant possibility; it is already reshaping how we communicate, decide, and even trust. The leaders who ignore it risk being left behind. The leaders who embrace it without reflection risk losing their authenticity.

The real challenge is clear: can trust-based leadership survive and even thrive in a world where machines now share the table with us?

CHAPTER 11

Artificial Intelligence and Trust-Based Leadership: Navigating the New Frontier

rtificial intelligence is not coming; it is already here, reshaping classrooms, boardrooms, and every corner of daily life. For many leaders, the question is no longer *if* AI will affect them, but *how quickly* and *at what cost*. I didn't first encounter this shift at a business conference or through an industry white paper. My introduction came in a much more personal way, through a conversation at home with my own children.

In early 2023, both my son and daughter came to me and told me about something called ChatGPT. They explained that students were starting to use it in school to write papers. My immediate reaction was to tell them not to use it; it felt like plagiarism, a shortcut that undermined real learning. At that time, I had no idea what artificial intelligence truly was, nor could I have predicted the profound impact tools like ChatGPT would soon have.

Shortly after my kids first brought AI to my attention, I decided to explore it myself, but with a very different mindset. I was determined to use it in the most honorable way. My first goal was not just to get help from AI; I wanted it to learn *who I am*. I fed it my writings, my ideas, my style of communication. I trained it to understand me, not just my words, but my principles, leadership approach, and way of thinking. If I was going to use AI in my work, it needed to reflect *my authentic self*, not sound like a generic robot from cyberspace. To accelerate that process, I often used my phone to record thoughts and decisions in real-time, speaking to it as though I were on a call. These recordings doubled as prompts—specific instructions that helped AI capture not only what I decided, but how I thought through problems. On one occasion, while dictating prompts in an elevator, a passerby overheard me and assumed I was being rude on the phone. They didn't realize I wasn't talking to a person at all—I was training an AI to mirror my decision-making process. At first, it was frustrating. No matter how much effort I put in, AI still went off script, generating responses that did not sound like me. But I kept refining it, teaching it, pushing it to align with my voice. Finally, about nine months into this experience, I asked it to draft my first email.

What happened next amazed me. The email *felt like me*. It was structured exactly how I would have written it, but instead of taking an hour to compose and send, AI delivered it in 30 seconds. That was the moment I realized AI was not just a shortcut; it was a powerful amplifier. It had the potential to enhance my efficiency while still preserving my authenticity.

This is where the story begins for me. The real question was: What next? How do we, as leaders, integrate AI in a way that strengthens rather than undermines trust? How do we navigate the new frontier where AI is not just a tool but a fundamental part of decision-making, communication, and leadership?

This chapter explores these questions, laying out the impact of AI on trust-based leadership and the strategies we need to maintain integrity in an AI-driven world.

Defining AI's Role in Authentic Leadership

AI has become an integral part of modern business leadership, offering tools that enhance efficiency, streamline decision-making, and optimize workflows. However, the rise of AI also presents a challenge. How can leaders ensure they remain authentic while integrating AI into their leadership practices? The key lies in viewing AI as an amplifier rather than a replacement for leadership qualities. AI should serve as a support system that enhances a leader's ability to connect with their team, communicate effectively, and make well-informed decisions, all while maintaining human intuition and empathy.

Yet, despite its potential, a significant degree of hesitation remains among leaders in adopting AI as a leadership tool. This reluctance often stems less from technical limitations and more from a psychological gap, rooted in unfamiliarity, fear of losing control, or dystopian narratives popularized by media (e.g., *The Terminator*). Leaders tend to approach AI with caution, often defaulting to worst-case scenarios rather than envisioning its current, practical use cases like digital twins, predictive analytics, and natural language processing that are already accelerating learning and decision-making at reduced costs.

Trust in AI is still developing. Research shows that while AI is perceived as highly capable in technical tasks, it consistently underperforms in perceived social skills, especially negotiation and social perceptiveness, which are vital for leadership credibility and team trust. Moreover, leaders may fear that integrating AI could depersonalize their communication or dilute the human-centered aspects of leadership.

This is where authentic leadership becomes essential. Trust in AI must be cultivated through human leadership by introducing, educating, and modeling its appropriate use within everyday workflows. Leaders who transparently incorporate AI tools, while explaining their benefits and limitations, are more likely to foster acceptance and build trust among their teams. As Aboumoussa and Pfister (2024) emphasize, leadership in the age of AI requires a mindset shift toward embracing AI as a co-pilot, with humans firmly in command of ethical, emotional, and strategic dimensions.

To retain authenticity, leaders must go beyond passive adoption of AI. They must actively train their AI tools to understand and reflect their values, voice, and leadership style, ensuring that every output generated aligns with the leader's own intent and ethical framework. This also entails preserving final oversight on AI-supported decisions. AI should be an extension of human judgment, not a substitute.

Books such as *AI 2041* by Kai-Fu Lee and Chen Qiufan, and *AI Superpowers* by Kai-Fu Lee, further stress the importance of proactive leadership in shaping AI's integration. They argue that trust and societal benefit will not emerge automatically but must be led by human intention, governance, and empathy.

Ultimately, the challenge is not whether AI can be used in leadership, but how it can be integrated in a way that strengthens, rather than compromises, the authenticity of the human leaders who wield it.

Servant Leadership and AI: How to Stay True to Your Leadership Values

Servant leadership is rooted in humility, empathy, and a deep commitment to the well-being and development of others. As artificial intelligence becomes increasingly present in the workplace, servant leaders face the unique challenge of adopting technology while staying true to these values. Done thoughtfully, AI can be a powerful enabler of servant leadership, enhancing communication, deepening listening, supporting fair decision-making, and amplifying mentorship.

Servant leaders prioritize meaningful relationships with their teams, and communication plays a critical role in building trust. AI can help leaders scale this communication without losing authenticity. For example, AI tools can help leaders draft personalized messages, automate routine updates, and generate insights for team recognition. The key, as highlighted by Ressem (2023), is ensuring that AI outputs reflect the leader's voice and tone, so that even automated messages feel personal and aligned with the leader's values.

Moreover, tools that analyze communication patterns or flag engagement trends enable leaders to act proactively, identifying team members who may require additional support or recognition. As Dorner (2024) notes, employees are more likely to trust AI-assisted communication when it's transparent, ethically guided, and clearly backed by human oversight.

One of the most essential behaviors in servant leadership is listening. AI can dramatically improve a leader's ability to listen at scale by analyzing employee feedback, conducting sentiment analysis, and surfacing recurring issues. These capabilities help leaders stay in tune with their teams' needs, especially in large or remote organizations.

However, as emphasized in the Harvard Kennedy School report by Aboumoussa and Pfister (2024), listening must be paired with action. AI can detect the signals, but leaders must respond with empathy and accountability. When team members see their input reflected in decisions or follow-up actions, trust in both leadership and the technology grows.

AI can support servant leaders by providing data-driven insights to inform decision-making. From resource allocation to team structuring, AI can offer pattern recognition and forecasts that enhance objectivity. Yet, servant leadership demands more than efficiency; it requires fairness, equity, and transparency. Servant leaders must ensure that AI tools do not perpetuate bias or undermine trust. As *AI Superpowers* highlights, leaders must remain accountable for the outputs and ensure human judgment remains central. Sharing how AI is used and involving team members in shaping its application, what Aboumoussa and Pfister call "digital co-leadership," reinforces a culture of trust and shared responsibility.

Finally, servant leaders are mentors and coaches. AI can extend this impact by providing customized learning paths, tracking development progress, and identifying career growth opportunities based on performance and aspirations. These tools, when guided by human empathy and leadership, can democratize access to mentorship and foster a culture of growth.

Still, mentorship remains a deeply human function. AI should not replace the relational aspects of growth conversations. Instead, it should empower leaders to make those interactions more informed and personalized. This aligns with the principles in *AI 2041*, which argues that the future of leadership lies in symbiotic relationships between human values and AI capabilities.

By using AI to enhance, not replace, the behaviors central to servant leadership, leaders can build more engaged, informed, and trusting teams. The opportunity is not in choosing between AI and empathy, but in designing systems where the two work hand in hand.

How AI Enhances Trust in Leadership

AI offers a unique opportunity to strengthen, not weaken, trust in leadership when implemented with transparency and human-centered values. Servant leadership emphasizes presence, accountability, and meaningful connection, and AI can support these ideals when used thoughtfully.

One of the most immediate benefits of AI is its ability to reduce administrative burdens. Tools that automate scheduling, summarize meeting notes, or draft standard communications can free up valuable time for leaders to focus on relationship-building, coaching, and strategic thinking. As noted by Aboumoussa and Pfister (2024), AI can "augment human leadership capacity" by allowing leaders to be more present with their teams.

Rather than replacing human involvement, AI should be positioned as a backend assistant, streamlining operational tasks so leaders can be more visible and engaged. This aligns closely with the servant leadership model, which prioritizes time spent supporting and listening to others.

Employees are more likely to accept AI-driven tools when they understand how they are used and see that human oversight is preserved. Transparency about AI's role in decision-making, performance evaluations, or communication creates confidence and reduces fear. Dorner (2024) emphasizes that trust in AI increases when leaders openly communicate its purpose and involve teams in the implementation process. Trust is further strengthened when leaders model ethical use of AI, ensuring that algorithms support fairness, do not introduce bias, and remain accountable to human values. Ressem (2023) warns that without this level of openness, AI risks becoming a perceived threat to authenticity and fairness in leadership. Servant leaders who make AI use visible and explainable help their teams understand it as a partner in progress, rather than a surveillance tool or decision-maker in disguise.

Ultimately, building trust with AI is less about the technology itself and more about how leaders guide its integration. Trust grows when employees see their leaders use AI to amplify human strengths, empathy, communication, and fairness, rather than bypass them. Servant leaders are uniquely positioned to lead this cultural shift, modeling both ethical stewardship and practical use of AI to foster trust across the organization.

Ethical AI Use: Avoiding Pitfalls That Undermine Trust

As AI tools become more deeply embedded in organizations, servant leaders must navigate a range of ethical considerations to ensure trust is upheld rather than eroded. The risks of over-automation, diminished human oversight, and compromised privacy are real, and avoiding these pitfalls requires intentionality, transparency, and strong values-based leadership.

Over-reliance on AI can undermine a leader's connection with their team. While AI can efficiently draft messages, schedule meetings, or provide routine feedback, it should never replace the relational aspects of leadership. In situations involving emotional nuance, such as employee recognition, conflict resolution, or crisis management, AI falls short. As emphasized in *AI Superpowers*, AI excels in efficiency but lacks the emotional depth necessary for complex human interaction. Servant leaders must ensure that human presence and empathy remain central, especially in moments that shape trust and team morale.

AI can analyze vast amounts of data, offering insights that would be impossible to process manually. However, these outputs must not be accepted blindly. Leaders must apply critical thinking and human judgment to every AI-generated recommendation. As Ressem (2023) notes, overdependence on AI can result in flawed or ethically questionable outcomes when algorithms are accepted without scrutiny.

Servant leaders must remain the ultimate decision-makers, using AI as a tool to inform rather than dictate.

AI systems that monitor employee behavior or performance must be implemented with care. Transparency is essential; employees need to know what data is being collected, how it is being used, and who has access to it. When AI is perceived as intrusive or controlling, it can quickly erode the culture of trust. Dorner (2024) highlights the importance of clarity and ethical boundaries in organizational AI use, emphasizing that trust depends not only on functionality but also on perceived fairness and respect for personal boundaries.

A servant leader prioritizes ethical AI governance by establishing clear, respectful guidelines for AI use, particularly when it involves sensitive information. This includes fostering an open dialogue about AI tools, addressing concerns, and involving employees in shaping how AI impacts their work. In doing so, leaders can ensure that AI remains a trusted aid, not a threat to autonomy or dignity.

The responsible use of AI starts with values. Ethical pitfalls can be avoided when leaders treat AI not as a shortcut, but as a tool to support thoughtful, human-centered leadership. By combining technical capability with emotional intelligence and moral judgment, servant leaders can ensure AI is used ethically to uplift both individuals and the organization.

The Future of AI in Servant Leadership: What's Next?

A decade ago, tacit objection modeling was focused on creating virtual clones of the best decision-makers, AI models that could emulate expert judgment under various scenarios. Today, however, the challenge has evolved beyond decision-making alone. Leaders must ensure that AI captures not only their logic but also their values, ethics, and leadership style —in essence, their authenticity.

In the modern AI landscape, the goal is no longer just to replicate decision-making prowess but to clone the essence of leadership itself. This means training AI models to reflect the leader's vision, communication style, and emotional intelligence while ensuring that AI-driven interactions remain true to the leader's core principles. By feeding AI with their own writings, recorded speeches, and decision-making patterns, leaders can create a virtual presence that enhances consistency and trust across digital interactions. However, this also requires careful governance to ensure AI does not distort, dilute, or over-automate leadership responsibilities.

As AI becomes more ingrained in leadership functions, the emphasis should be on authentic augmentation rather than replacement. Leaders must design AI models that enhance their leadership capabilities while preserving the human connection that defines strong leadership. The process of cloning leadership for AI should be approached with a servant leadership mindset, ensuring that AI tools serve to empower teams rather than reduce leadership to automated outputs.

AI 2041: Ten Visions for Our Future presents a compelling look at how AI is set to change society, businesses, and leadership. One of the key takeaways is that AI will not replace human leaders but rather augment them. The book emphasizes that AI should be designed to work alongside humans, complementing human strengths while mitigating weaknesses.

For business leaders, this means that AI should not be seen as an all-powerful decision-maker but as an enabler of more efficient, ethical, and personalized leadership. The book also highlights the risks of algorithmic bias and the ethical implications of AI-driven decision-making, reinforcing the need for leaders to implement AI systems that prioritize fairness, inclusivity, and transparency.

A key lesson from *AI 2041* is that while AI can handle data-driven decisions at scale, true leadership requires emotional intelligence, moral judgment, and human connection—traits that AI cannot replicate. This aligns with the principles of servant leadership, where leaders act as stewards of their organizations, ensuring that AI is used responsibly to benefit employees, customers, and society as a whole.

Kai-Fu Lee's *AI Superpowers: China, Silicon Valley, and the New World Order* provides another crucial perspective on the rapid development of AI and its impact on leadership. One of the book's most important lessons is the difference between the AI-driven economic transformation in the West versus China, highlighting the importance of adaptability and resilience in leadership.

For servant leaders, the book underscores that while AI can drive efficiency, automation, and scalability, true leadership remains human-centric. The most successful AI-powered organizations, according to *AI Superpowers*, are those that combine AI's capabilities with strong empathy, vision, and personal relationships. Lee argues that compassion, trust, and social responsibility must be at the forefront of leadership in the AI era.

Another key takeaway from the book is the importance of AI-powered innovation and the necessity of lifelong learning for leaders. In a rapidly evolving technological landscape, leaders must continuously upskill, embrace AI as a strategic partner, and foster a growth mindset in their organizations. This lines up with the concept of servant leadership, where leaders prioritize the development of their teams, ensuring they are equipped with the tools and knowledge to thrive in an AI-driven world.

As AI capabilities grow more sophisticated, it is tempting to envision a future where machines assume leadership roles. However, the most powerful and sustainable model is one where AI serves as a strategic assistant, not a replacement, for human leadership. AI can automate repetitive tasks, generate insights from vast data sets, and support decision-making with speed and precision. But the essence of leadership, empathy, moral judgment, mentorship, and vision, remains inherently human.

Servant leaders who embrace AI with this perspective gain a critical advantage. They can delegate operational complexity to AI, freeing themselves to focus on more human-centered responsibilities such as guiding teams, nurturing culture, and resolving conflicts with compassion. This balance not only enhances productivity but also reinforces trust. According to *AI 2041*, organizations that thrive in the future will be those that leverage AI to augment, rather than replace, human leadership, creating hybrid systems where machines support and humans lead.

AI has the potential to promote equity and inclusion in the workplace by minimizing human bias in decisions such as hiring, promotions, and performance evaluations. When designed and deployed thoughtfully, AI systems can serve as fairness accelerators, identifying systemic imbalances, flagging inconsistencies, and offering objective recommendations.

However, this potential can only be realized if leaders remain actively involved in governing how these tools are used. As Ressem (2023) and Dorner (2024) caution, algorithms can reflect and even amplify existing societal biases if left unchecked. Leaders must take responsibility for the ethical oversight of AI, ensuring that models are trained on diverse data, that decision-making processes are transparent, and that the final judgment always includes human review.

Inclusive leadership in the AI era entails balancing technological advancements with social responsibility. It means using AI not just to improve efficiency, but to elevate the values of fairness and belonging that lie at the heart of servant leadership.

The accelerating pace of AI innovation requires leaders to evolve constantly. To remain effective, servant leaders must be committed to continuous learning, not only of technological tools but of their ethical and organizational implications. This mindset of lifelong learning and adaptability is critical for future-proofing leadership. Kai-Fu Lee, in *AI Superpowers*, underscores the importance of combining technical literacy with soft skills like empathy, creativity, and resilience. The leaders who will thrive in an AI-driven world are those who can straddle both domains: embracing the benefits of automation while reinforcing the uniquely human aspects of leadership.

To achieve this, leaders must foster a culture of digital curiosity within their organizations. They must empower their teams to explore and use AI tools safely and ethically, while modeling transparency, fairness, and humility. By cultivating a learning mindset and anchoring it in core leadership values, servant leaders will ensure that their organizations are not just AI-ready but values-driven and trust-centered.

Final Takeaway

Servant leaders must view AI as a tool to enhance trust, empathy, and efficiency, rather than as a replacement for genuine, human-centered leadership that teams rely on. The key lies in intentionality. AI must be purposefully integrated into leadership practices to serve as an amplifier of human values, not a substitute for them. Leaders must approach AI with clarity about its role, consistently ensuring that its use aligns with the organization's mission, ethical principles, and communication culture. When used this way, AI can remove friction from workflows, help leaders connect with more people more effectively, and reinforce consistency in how values are demonstrated across the organization.

However, the path forward requires humility, transparency, and an unwavering commitment to authenticity. Trust will not be built by technology alone; it will be earned through human leadership that models how to use AI responsibly and ethically. Servant leaders are uniquely positioned to guide this evolution. By staying grounded in their values, remaining accountable, and actively involving their teams in AI integration, they can ensure that the future of leadership remains as personal and principled as ever, even as it becomes more digitally empowered.

Yet whether we are talking about the newest technology or the oldest principles of human connection, one truth remains: trust must be lived out daily. It cannot be reduced to strategies or systems alone; it must be experienced. To see how this plays out in practice, we now turn to *The Experience*, a 360° perspective on how trust manifests among employees, clients, and leaders alike.

PART III Future:

Sustaining Trust-Based Leadership

CHAPTER 12

The Experience: A 360° Perspective

Trust is the bedrock of any thriving organization, and *The Experience* exemplifies how a culture rooted in trust can create unparalleled success. Over the years, as a company, we grappled with finding the right terminology to define our way of working. For a long time, we referred to our approach as "culture," a term that was widely accepted but often misused or misunderstood within the industry. Culture seemed abstract, overused, and burdened with connotations that failed to fully capture the essence of what we were striving to achieve.

Through countless discussions and reflections, we realized that *"The Experience"* was the term that truly resonated. Unlike culture, which can feel static or misaligned, experience embodies the dynamic, vibrant, and tangible moments that define daily life within an organization. The word experience captures the reality of how employees, clients, and partners interact with the company—how they feel, what they achieve, and how they grow in the process.

This shift in terminology represented a fundamental shift for us. For example, as we transitioned from talking about "culture" to "experience," it became clearer that our focus was not on a theoretical framework but on the actual lived moments that make up organizational life. When an employee participates in our Idea Pitch process or engages in cross-functional collaboration, they're not merely conforming to a cultural norm; they're actively shaping and living an experience. Similarly, when a client places trust in our ability to deliver solutions, they're not aligning with an abstract ideal but engaging in a real, impactful interaction.

This new perspective energized our approach to leadership and organizational growth. *The Experience* became a driving force behind everything we do, aligning the company's spirit with its actions. It transformed the abstract into the tangible, creating a cohesive and actionable framework that empowers employees, delights clients, and fosters partnerships. By focusing on the now and embracing a high-energy, purpose-driven mindset, we set the stage for innovation, trust, and excellence.

Through this chapter, I aim to explore the core principles and practices that define *The Experience* and how it integrates into every aspect of our work. *The Experience* is not just a strategy—it is a way of being, a testament to the power of trust in action, and a blueprint for organizations seeking to inspire, grow, and achieve at the highest levels.

A Leadership Moment That Changed Me

One of the most formative leadership experiences I've had didn't happen in a boardroom or during a high-stakes negotiation. It happened in the hallway of one of our client sites, sparked by an offhand comment that could have easily gone unnoticed.

At the time, we were in the middle of supporting a large-scale transformation effort for a key client; an initiative that required us to go beyond technical consulting and really listen to the voice of the frontline staff. Our team had built a framework to capture that voice systematically by gathering feedback, analyzing trends, and providing leadership with clear, actionable insights. It was one of those efforts that had taken months to refine, and the client was genuinely excited about it.

But one afternoon, during a site visit, I heard that someone from our own team had made a dismissive remark about the effort, not to the client, but within earshot of our other consultants. It was a subtle sarcastic comment about whether the feedback would ever be taken seriously. But it stuck. I could feel the shift in energy among the team. Something was off.

I didn't confront it immediately. I wanted to understand what was going on beneath the surface. A few days later, I received an internal memo: a formal justification of the initiative's validity, complete with references to contract language and alignment with the client's goals. It was professionally done. But it read more like a defense brief than a reflection. What it didn't say was why this memo needed to exist in the first place. No names were mentioned, but everyone involved knew who and what it was about.

That's when I realized the deeper issue wasn't the comment or the memo—it was the erosion of trust inside our own team. And if I let it go, I'd be complicit in allowing that erosion to spread.

So, I invited the key people involved into a conversation. Not a reprimand. Not a review. A real, human conversation.

I began by identifying what I had observed: the impact of that one comment, how it altered the room's tone, and how it eroded the integrity of something the team had worked so hard to establish. Then I asked a question that changed the whole tone: "If you had questions or concerns, why didn't you bring them forward earlier, directly and respectfully? What kept you from doing that?"

What followed was a moment of honesty. The individual who made the comment admitted they were frustrated, not with the program itself, but with how stretched they felt and how uncertain they were that the client would act on the recommendations. Another team member said they hadn't felt safe enough to push back or ask clarifying questions when the framework was being rolled out. These weren't bad people. These were good people caught in the tension between performance pressure and psychological safety.

We talked about how easy it is to let doubt fester when we're overwhelmed. And how important it is, as professionals and as teammates, to check in with each other—not just on *what* we're doing, but *how* we're doing.

That conversation didn't fix everything overnight. But it was a turning point. The individual who had made the comment apologized—not because they were forced to, but because they came to understand the broader impact of their words. The memo writer, who had tried to protect the work with formal language, realized that technical justifications can't rebuild trust; only relationships can. And as a team, we agreed to shift how we bring concerns forward: directly, openly, and with the assumption of good intent.

For me, it was a powerful reminder that leadership is not about controlling outcomes. It's about creating space—especially when things feel uncomfortable—for people to be real, to be heard, and to be part of the solution.

That's what *The Experience* is all about. It's not a process or a policy. It's what lives in the spaces between people: the tone in a meeting, the intention behind feedback, the way we own our mistakes. And it's in those moments, more than any dashboard or deliverable, where trust is either reinforced or quietly broken.

That experience changed me. It made me more present, more aware, and more committed to leading in a way that heals and builds, not just manages and measures. It showed me that trust isn't built during the easy times. It's built in how we show up during the hard ones.

Employees: Empowerment with Accountability

Employees are the heart of *The Experience*. They define the rhythm of the organization through their actions, ideas, and attitudes. But empowerment, if not grounded in accountability, quickly becomes chaos or entitlement. True empowerment is not about giving people free rein—it's about giving them ownership. It means trusting them with decisions, encouraging initiative, and allowing room for creativity, while also holding them to high standards of performance and integrity.

In our company, we've seen the difference it makes when employees feel heard, valued, and challenged. Programs like Idea Pitch aren't just exercises in engagement; they are affirmations of trust. When people are permitted to lead from where they are, innovation flourishes. But this only works if the environment supports feedback loops, clarity of expectations, and the psychological safety to admit mistakes and grow.

Servant leadership shows up here not through control, but through service by removing roadblocks, offering guidance, and modeling the accountability we expect in return. When employees experience trust, autonomy, and meaningful responsibility, they don't just work for the company—they *become* the company.

Clients: Excellence as a Relationship, Not a Transaction

Clients are not simply recipients of our services; they are co-creators of the outcome. Every touchpoint with a client—whether it's an email, a status update, or a leadership briefing—is an opportunity to reinforce trust or erode it. That's why we approach excellence not as a checklist, but as a relationship.

Delivering on scope and schedule is expected. What distinguishes *The Experience* is how we listen, adapt, and show up with transparency. Clients remember when we own our missteps. They notice when we anticipate their needs instead of reacting. And they develop loyalty not just because of what we do, but because of how we make them feel.

We've had clients tell us that what kept them with us wasn't just our technical expertise but the consistency, empathy, and care we brought to every interaction. *That's the core of client excellence:* making trust tangible, service personal, and every engagement a reflection of our values.

Partners: Trust Beyond the Contract

In today's interconnected landscape, very few projects are delivered alone. We depend on subcontractors, teaming partners, and collaborators who operate outside our org chart but are fully embedded in our mission. These partners represent our company when we're not in the room. And yet, in many organizations, they're treated as secondary.

Not here.

We've learned that if we want partners to act like insiders, we have to treat them like insiders. That means sharing information openly, listening to their input, aligning goals, and extending the same level of trust we reserve for internal teams. It also means having the tough conversations when expectations aren't met, but doing so with dignity and a focus on mutual growth.

When partnerships are built on transactional thinking, they crumble under stress. But when they are built on shared values and mutual respect, they become one of the strongest elements of *The Experience.*

Our best partner relationships feel like extensions of our team—and our clients can feel that cohesion.

Leaders: Modeling the Culture We Want

Leadership is not about status or control. It's about setting the tone, creating the environment, and embodying the values that we want to see replicated across the organization. In *The Experience*, leadership means showing up authentically, especially when things are uncertain or uncomfortable.

Employees watch how leaders respond to mistakes. Clients notice how we handle feedback. Partners evaluate whether we walk our talk. In all these cases, the leader's behavior either reinforces trust or breaks it.

What I've learned over the years is that consistency matters more than charisma. Leaders don't need to have all the answers, but they do need to be visible, responsive, and real. They need to admit when they're wrong. They need to listen deeply. And they need to act in alignment with the company's values—not just when it's easy, but especially when it's not.

In servant leadership, authority is earned through service, not asserted through hierarchy. When leaders model vulnerability, accountability, and presence, they inspire others to do the same. That's when trust becomes systemic.

Having seen how trust takes root in relationships across every level of an organization, the questions become: *How do we ensure it endures? How do we carry this forward into the future, where new challenges, new contexts, and new generations will continue to test it?* That is the focus of the next chapter.

CHAPTER 13

The Journey Continues

L eadership is not a destination. It is a living practice; a commitment renewed with every interaction, every decision, and every challenge. While the earlier chapters of this book introduced tools, strategies, and frameworks for building trust-based and servant leadership cultures, this chapter provides an opportunity to pause, reflect, and consider the road ahead.

The journey we've taken together has not been linear. We began by exploring what trust truly means in a world where it is often broken before it is built. We then expanded that definition to encompass the 360-degree nature of trust—between leaders and teams, peers, clients, and most importantly, within ourselves. We discussed how burnout and misalignment can take root when people operate too long outside their zone of purpose and strength. We examined the 80/20 alignment, the Red-Yellow-Green energy mapping, and the 4Cs—Commitment, Courage, Capability, and Confidence—as tools to help people and organizations operate more intentionally and more humanely.

Each chapter asked us to consider a fundamental question: *What kind of experience are we creating for others and for ourselves through the way we lead?*

The answer, again and again, pointed back to trust. Not as a vague ideal, but as a practice. Not as a bonus, but as the foundation.

Trust is not something we give once. It is something we build slowly, sometimes painfully, over time, and sometimes we're asked to rebuild it in places we thought were long closed. This is true in leadership. And it's true in life.

Not long ago, I was reminded just how deep trust can go. There are moments when a relationship you thought belonged only to the past reappears unexpectedly, offering a second chance. Years—even decades—may pass, yet the emotions, memories, and lessons resurface as if no time had gone by. What once seemed permanently closed reveals itself as a door that had only been waiting. And in that moment, trust becomes more than a professional principle; it becomes a profoundly human experience.

Sometimes it only takes a quiet message or a small gesture to reopen a door we thought was closed. What begins as a simple exchange can grow into a series of honest conversations, a reconnection that feels both familiar and entirely new. The goal isn't to return to the past, but to honor it while meeting each other as who we have become. In those moments of walking forward together, we often find ourselves living the very questions this book has explored: *How do we rebuild trust? How do we lead with authenticity? And how do we embrace the doors that open when we least expect them?*

Could I show up with vulnerability, not just as a leader, but as a man? Could I take accountability for the things I didn't say all those years ago? Could I trust—not with blind hope, but with clear eyes and an open heart?

In that experience, I came face-to-face with the real work of leadership: listening, forgiving, staying present, and being brave enough to begin again. The very same principles that build high-performing teams also heal relationships. The same empathy that transforms a workplace can resurrect something thought lost. I realized that leadership is not just about projects, metrics, or vision boards, but about presence and how we choose to show up in the lives of others.

Sometimes the most powerful doors are not the ones we walk through in triumph, but the ones we walk back through with humility.

This is the essence of trust-based leadership: not perfection, but presence. Not dominance, but dialogue. Not control, but connection.

And so, it continues.

There is no finish line in this kind of leadership. There is only deepening of clarity, conviction, and courage. Whether you're running a company, raising a family, mentoring a team, or finding your way back to a lost love, the principles remain the same. Trust is the soil. Relationships are the roots. Growth is the outcome.

If there's one lesson I hope stays with you from this book, it is this: you don't need to have all the answers to be a great leader. But you do need to be willing to ask better questions. You don't need to always be right, but you do need to be real.

And above all, remember that some of the most important doors you'll ever walk through are the ones that wait.

As we look ahead, the process does not end—it deepens. I would like to leave you with one final invitation: to reclaim the 20% that has the power to transform not only your leadership, but the way you live.

CHAPTER 14

Conclusion

Trust-based leadership transcends traditional models by emphasizing relationships, understanding, and mutual respect. But it is not simply a new leadership style—it is a mindset. A calling. A commitment to lead with presence, not position; with courage, not control; and with empathy, not ego.

Throughout this book, we have explored how trust transforms teams, cultures, and lives. We've seen that trust is not a soft concept; it is a strategic imperative. It shapes how decisions are made, how problems are solved, and how people show up for one another. In times of crisis, trust creates stability. In times of change, it fuels innovation. And in moments of doubt, it becomes the tether that holds people together.

But building trust is not easy. It requires leaders to be vulnerable enough to admit what they don't know, and secure enough to share what they do. It asks us to listen when we'd rather speak, to empower when we're tempted to control, and to serve even when recognition may never come. These are not traits we simply adopt; they are capacities we develop over time, through experience, humility, and reflection.

The real challenge of trust-based leadership is that it is not situational—it is constant. It's not something we turn on when things are going well.

It is what we return to when things fall apart. It is the foundation we build *before* the storm, so that when the winds come, our people have something solid to stand on.

In today's world, where organizations face unprecedented complexity and workers are seeking more meaning, belonging, and purpose, the call for a new kind of leadership has never been clearer. We must lead with authenticity. We must lead with intention. We must lead with trust.

This book is not the final word. It is a guide, a starting point, a conversation. The true work begins now, in your daily choices and quiet moments. Whether you are a CEO, a manager, a founder, or someone just stepping into leadership, you hold the power to shape the experience of those around you.

So, ask yourself often:

- Am I building or eroding trust right now?
- Am I leading from a place of fear or from a place of service?
- What kind of legacy do I want to leave—not in words, but in the stories others tell about working with me?

Because in the end, that is what leadership is. Not a role. Not a title. But an experience.

One shaped by how deeply we choose to care and how bravely we choose to lead.

The journey continues.

And the door is open.

The Quiet Door

I've come to believe that some of the most important doors in life don't slam shut or swing wide open—they wait. Quietly. Without pressure or expectation. They wait for us to become ready. To notice. To return with new eyes.

Writing this book was its own kind of door. It asked me to stop, to remember, and to tell the truth. Not just about what I've learned as a leader, but about who I've become as a man. And as I reflect on this undertaking—not just across the chapters, but across decades—I see one thread running through it all: the power of choosing trust. Over and over again.

Trust in others. Trust in change. Trust in love. Trust, even when we've been hurt.
Especially then.

If you're holding this book, there's probably a door in your life, too. One you're approaching. One you're afraid to open. Or one you never thought would open again.

You don't need to force it. You don't need to have all the answers.

You just need to take the next step with presence, courage, and the belief that sometimes...what's waiting on the other side is not what you lost, but what you've grown enough to finally receive.

So wherever this book finds you,
In a quiet evening office
At a turning point in your career,
Or just holding a question you can't yet answer,
Know this:

The door is still there.
And you are not alone.

About the Author

Ivan Radovic is a global business leader, strategist, and lifelong student of trust. As President of NOVACES, LLC, a firm specializing in performance improvement, disaster recovery, and government consulting, Ivan has spent over two decades leading teams through complexity and change. From military healthcare systems to disaster zones, from corporate boardrooms to federal agencies, he has helped organizations find clarity, restore stability, and build lasting cultures rooted in purpose.

Born in Prague, Czech Republic and raised in the former Yugoslavia, Ivan came to the United States in the early 1990s after witnessing the collapse of trust in society during the Balkan wars. He worked multiple jobs while putting himself through college and eventually built a successful career helping others rebuild from the inside out. His leadership philosophy is shaped by both Eastern European realism and American possibility, always returning to one core idea: trust is not a soft skill—it's the foundation of everything.

Ivan is also a father, a facilitator, a mentor, and a passionate believer in second chances. His work with entrepreneurs through the Entrepreneurs' Organization (EO), along with the culture he continues to shape at NOVACES, reflects his commitment to servant leadership, vulnerability, and human connection.

This book is a culmination of lessons lived and learned, but not the end of the conversation. Ivan's next project, *Open Door Theory*, continues the journey, exploring how we make the pivotal choices that shape our leadership and our lives. It invites us to stay open to new possibilities, to notice the doors already within reach, rather than walking familiar but misguided paths. Not all closed doors are meant to stay shut; some are waiting patiently for us to find the courage to open them.

References

Leadership, Trust, and Organizational Development

Blanchard, Ken, and Phil Hodges. Lead Like Jesus: Lessons from the Greatest Leadership Role Model of All Time. Thomas Nelson, 2005.

Covey, Stephen M.R. The Speed of Trust: The One Thing That Changes Everything. Free Press, 2006.

Greenleaf, Robert K. Servant Leadership: A Journey into the Nature of Legitimate Power and Greatness. Paulist Press, 1977.

Kahneman, Daniel. Thinking, Fast and Slow. Farrar, Straus and Giroux, 2011.

Lencioni, Patrick. The Five Dysfunctions of a Team: A Leadership Fable. Jossey-Bass, 2002.

Lencioni, Patrick. The 6 Types of Working Genius: A Better Way to Understand Your Gifts, Your Frustrations, and Your Team. Matt Holt Books, 2020.

Lencioni, Patrick. Getting Naked: A Business Fable About Shedding The Three Fears That Sabotage Client Loyalty. Jossey-Bass, 2010.

Marcus Buckingham & Donald O. Clifton. Now, Discover Your Strengths. Free Press, 2001.

McKeown, Greg. Essentialism: The Disciplined Pursuit of Less. Crown Business, 2014.

Pink, Daniel H. Drive: The Surprising Truth About What Motivates Us. Riverhead Books, 2009.

Porter, Michael E. What Is Strategy? Harvard Business Review, November–December 1996.

Rath, Tom. StrengthsFinder 2.0. Gallup Press, 2007.

Sinek, Simon. Leaders Eat Last: Why Some Teams Pull Together and Others Don't. Portfolio, 2014.

Sullivan, Dan, & Hardy, Benjamin. 10x Is Easier Than 2x: How World-Class Entrepreneurs Achieve More by Doing Less. Hay House Business, 2023.

Tzu, Sun. The Art of War. Translated by Lionel Giles, various editions.

Artificial Intelligence and Leadership Ethics

Aboumoussa, A., & Pfister, A. (2024). Leadership development in the age of AI. Harvard Kennedy School. https://www.hks.harvard.edu

Brynjolfsson, Erik, and Andrew McAfee. The Second Machine Age: Work, Progress, and Prosperity in a Time of Brilliant Technologies. W. W. Norton & Company, 2014.

Choudhury, Prithwiraj. AI and the Future of Work. Harvard Business Review, July–August 2023.

Dorner, S. (2024). Public perception of artificial intelligence: Trust, skills, and expectations. Journal of Organizational Behavior and Technology, 15(1), 23–41.

Floridi, Luciano, and Josh Cowls. A Unified Framework of Five Principles for AI in Society. Harvard Data Science Review, 2021.

Lee, Kai-Fu, & Qiufan, C. AI 2041: Ten Visions for Our Future. Currency, 2021.

Lee, Kai-Fu. AI Superpowers: China, Silicon Valley, and the New World Order. Houghton Mifflin Harcourt, 2018.

Marcus, Gary, and Ernest Davis. Rebooting AI: Building Artificial Intelligence We Can Trust. Pantheon, 2019.

Ressem, L. (2023). Implementing AI in organizations: The role of leaders and impact on leadership. European Journal of Management and Technology, 12(4), 98–112.

Russell, Stuart. Human Compatible: Artificial Intelligence and the Problem of Control. Viking, 2019.

Siau, Keng, and Long Chen. A Call for AI Ethics in Business. International Journal of Artificial Intelligence & Applications, 2020.

World Economic Forum. Responsible Use of Technology: The Microsoft Case Study. WEF White Paper, 2022.

Frameworks and Concepts Referenced

80/20 Principle (Pareto Principle). Applied to personal energy and leadership task alignment.

AI and Authentic Leadership. Concepts presented by the author during the Global AI for Sustainable Business Conference in Dubai (2025), integrating AI decision augmentation with trust-based servant leadership.

Hidden Gems Brainstorming Exercise. Original tool for surfacing underutilized ideas and people.

Red-Yellow-Green Energy Mapping. A Visual tool adapted from NOVACES methodologies.

Servant Leadership Principles. Based on Robert Greenleaf's work, adapted to modern organizational settings.

The 4Cs Framework: Commitment, Courage, Capability, Confidence. Used to support trust-based performance conversations.

Trust 360 Model. The author's original framework. It illustrates multi-directional trust in organizations.

www.ingramcontent.com/pod-product-compliance
Lightning Source LLC
Chambersburg PA
CBHW031520120626
46545CB00005B/1922